Ground Cover

MINEKE KURPERSHOEK

INTRODUCTION BY RICHARD ROSENFELD

REBO
PRODUCTIONS

© 1995 Zuid Boekprodukties, Lisse
© 1997 Published by Rebo Productions Ltd
Text: Mineke Kurpershoek
Cover design and layout: Ton Wienbelt, The Netherlands
Photo editing: TextCase, The Netherlands
Production: TextCase, The Netherlands
Translation: Mary Boorman for first Edition Translations Ltd
Typesetting: Hof & Land Typografie, The Netherlands

ISBN 1 901094 41 3

Contents

Introduction

*Ground-cover plants are the unacknowledged heroes of the garden.
It's partly because the name sounds so splendidly disparaging and
unappetizing, so totally lacking in style, and partly because the
wicked mischievous snob in us thinks we are just too good for them.
How wrong,* Oh how wrong *can you be.*

*A guide to the new gardener goes like this. Visit the amazing famous
gardens, from Italy to California, draw up an impeccable plant list,
work out where you want to grow them, design the garden round the
plants, chopping and changing a few. Then the fun starts.*

*Though no gardening book ever says so, gardening can be
thunderingly expensive. So, very quickly, the moment you buy a
plant, you start working out how can I divide it?, making one into five.
Then you realize some plants are on your side. They actually
understand. They are very good spreaders. Scatter a few in an area and
let them get on with it, freeing you to whip up some start
arrangements. Nothing wrong with that. But what you forget is the
fast, thick spreaders are you doing aan extra service. The are keeping
down the weeds, and creating a natural mulch.*

*I remember facing a huge tumbling bank in my garden, made of solid
clay, that had once been thick with weeds. I had a go at planting some
comfrey. It didn't just say thank you very much, was soon striding
acros the garden, climbing sheer walls, and making for the lane.
Which is the real trick in arranging your ground cover; making sure it
does not go beserk.*

*Mineke Kurpershoek's book ought to come free with every plant. It
tackles the all-time favourites like* Vinca major *as well as woodland
perennials like waldsteinia, with it's saucer-shaped yellow flowers,
and the astonishing trifolium, which grows in most of the world in
meadows and on scree, and has curious rounded leaves. It even
highlights plants that ought to be in any collection. Plants like*
Heuchera micrantha *'Palace Purple' which has gorgeous bronze-red,
metallic leaves, topped by whitish flowers, and the pink-flowering*
Geranium macrorrhizum *'Ingwersen's Variety'. And best of all, if you
like informal planting, with daisy-like flowers sprouting out of walls
and steps,* Erigeron karvinskianus.

*My only tip, to add to Mineke Kurpershoek's bright, lively text, is that
you should never let the likes of* Alchemilla mollis *anywhere near a
vegetable patch. I once idiotically watched it spread up a gravel path
to a strawberry bed. Thinking it rather fun and very chic, I ignored it,
until one day discovered it not only amongst the plants, but self-
seeding inside the clumps. There is, let me warn you, no way of getting
them out. You can wiggle around with a fork, and tweak them with
spoons and knives, but not all the kitchen armory will rid a strawberry
of such an invader. In the right place, ground-cover is fine. In the
wrong – it smiles like the devil.*

Richard Rosenfeld, East Sussex, 1997

What are ground-cover plants?

Strictly speaking ground-cover plants are plants or shrubs which grow along the surface of the ground and form a carpet covering the soil.

Ground cover is also provided by plants that have underground runners which produce new shoots or, in the case of ferns, the leaves. This gives a compact growth and a tangle of roots which often makes it impossible for other plants to become established.

Plants can also make surface runners which root in contact with the ground. Ivy, *Hedera*, and periwinkle, *Vinca*, are good examples. These runners can make new plants at the nodes — that is, where the leaves join the stem. These plantlets grow into full-sized plants which then repeat the process. This provides a dense carpet. The strawberry is a good example. The new plantlets can be separated from the parent plant and put elsewhere in the garden. There are also of course plants that seed freely and can form a thick carpet in that way.

This book describes not only the true ground-cover plants, but also the plants that are low growing and form a close carpet of leaves with their clumps. Lady's mantle *(Alchemilla)*, *Geranium* species, and catmint *(Nepeta)* are good examples. This last group, of which the perennials form an important part, also includes several shrubs, climbers, and conifers, not forgetting roses. Besides the very low, creeping shrubs there is a group of shrubs, which, in spite of the fact that they can reach a metre (three feet) in height, are included in this book. They are

shrubs which form a close, impenetrable structure with their spreading growth and branches which arch over or grow almost horizontally. A choice has had to be made from the selection currently available because there is so much on offer in well-stocked garden centres.

Ground cover in garden design

Ground-cover plants are indispensable in contemporary garden design. Until recently every garden had a lawn — even if only the size of a pocket handkerchief — but lawns are now more and more being replaced by ground cover. A lawn is rather static, its trimmed edges forming a sharp division between grass and the borders. For small, and even sometimes bigger children, you cannot do without a lawn. They can play on it without doing too much damage and that is impossible with ground cover. There are tough plants that can be walked on now and then without suffering too much but they are not suitable for romping around on. Many a gardener wants grass in his or her garden because, so they say, grass has a bright colour and gives a feeling of space. Against this it can be said that there are sufficient ground-cover plants with bright green foliage which grow to the same height as a well-mown lawn. Furthermore, many ground-cover plants do flower, some very profusely.

Grass forms the best known and toughest ground cover. Here there is a beautiful mown path between uncut grass.

In the wild, moss is the natural ground cover.

7

Pachysandra *and*
Geranium
maccrorhizum *make*
good cover for level
areas.

There is a large number of evergreen ground-cover plants and this can be the reason, too, for replacing the grass with ground cover. The advantage of the ground cover is that more species can be chosen, so that the different surfaces merge into each other in a natural, often surprising, way. The different leaf structures, height, flower shapes, and flower colours make a ground cover of perennials and shrubs much more exciting than a smooth green lawn.

Apart from replacing grass, ground-cover plants can be used on any area where you want a low planting. Ground cover forms a lovely carpet between tall and low shrubs, and under trees. Different kinds of ground cover can transform a slope into a fascinating piece of garden and they form the link between groups of taller plants in the border.

In short, ground-cover plants are especially attractive plants which can be used in many places in the garden. There is a wide range of shapes and colours.

Plant names

Only the gardener who is able to spend a lot of time on plants and who regularly looks things up in books and visits nurseries frequently will be familiar with plant names and not have too many problems with all that Latin. Plants have to have universally understood names and these are given in Latin. The

Plant a circle of
Lamiastrum *around a*
pear tree or a circle of
golden marjoram
around an apple tree.

scientific names are therefore the same throughout the world, while the common names vary from country to country and often even from region to region. There are even plants which have ten or more common names in one country. If you don't go to the nurseryman with a Latin name, but to a garden centre with just the common name, you are likely to be misled. What should have been a beautiful, round-headed maple with green leaves turns out in the spring to be a variegated cultivar, albeit round-headed. Had the gardener taken the Latin name to a nurseryman, the latter would have known exactly which shape and leaf colour was meant. Simply put: a 'Golden Delicious' is an apple, but not every apple is a 'Golden Delicious.'

In this book you will regularly come across words such as genus, species, variety, and cultivar, which is short for cultural variety. If we take the hosta, then it appears that this belongs to the family *Liliaceae*. Apart from the hosta this family also includes, for instance, asparagus, the onion, the day lily, and, of course, the lily itself. The name of the genus is *Hosta*, then comes the specific name, for example *fortunei*. There are, however, different cultivated varieties, all with a different appearance. These are given a third name, which is the cultivar. A cultivar is also called a cultivated form. *Hosta fortunei*

Hosta fortunei *'Obscura' has quite large leaves.*

9

'Obscura' is a cultivated form with a rather dark-green leaf which is quite broad, and pale mauve flowers. *Hosta fortunei* 'Moerheim' has green leaves with a white edge and pale lilac flowers. There can be no confusion about which is which.

The cultivars are therefore forms which have arisen through selective breeding. Varieties, abbreviated to "var.", are plants which have arisen naturally and have a form which is different from the original one. The names of genus, species, and variety are written in italics. The cultivar name is always put in single inverted commas, and always begins with a capital letter. From time to time you will come across a name preceded by "syn.", which is short for synonym. This means that the plant is also known by another name. You can well understand the confusion that arises because the experts from all over the world seem to go on discussing this sort of thing for ever. Fortunately there are publications which help — the RHS Plant Finder, which is published annually, gives an up to date list of plants with their correct names and which nurseries stock them.

Plant combinations for normal garden soil

A wide range of plants can be grown in a garden with well-drained soil, and the possibilities as far as ground cover is concerned are quite large.

Normal garden soil has been well dug and has an open texture so that the water can drain away readily. The soil must not be too dry and must contain some humus. Remember that the ground under trees and shrubs and along hedges and walls can stay relatively dry, so the planting must be adapted to the conditions or there must be a regular addition of compost or peat to raise the humus level. An annual dressing with fertilizer is desirable. Suggestions are given below for combining ground-cover plants with, here and there, the inclusion of other plants.

Creeping jenny, Lysimachia nummularia, *as ground cover between tall ornamental grasses and low bamboo.*

Sun lovers For normal garden soil with a sunny position the choice of plants and shrubs is very wide, and that applies to ground-cover plants too. It is only possible to make a few suggestions for combinations of plants because of the large number available. Different plants will also be included under other headings, because there are plants which tolerate full sun as well as light shade, or which thrive in another type of soil, such as the pirri-pirri-bur (*Acaena*), which will grow in sandy soil, if it is not too poor, as well as normal garden soil.

The lowest layer The very low-growing ground-cover plants, species that do not grow more than 5cm (2in) high, are the most suitable for

planting large areas around the terrace, along paths, and between stepping stones. For sunny positions make a selection from several cultivars of pirri-pirri-bur, button-weed, creeping jenny, self-heal, saxifrage, clover, knotweed, veronica and the rather taller violets. They all have a very low growth habit but they differ from each other in character. Some are rather succulent and others have a more dried-up look about them. They are not all suitable for growing together. The more succulent plants such as button-weed (*Cotula*), creeping jenny (*Lysimachia nummularia*), saxifrage (*Saxifraga arendsii* hybrids), and veronica (*Veronica repens*) go well together and can be filled in with the pretty variegated clover (*Trifolium repens*), several groups of violets, and a ground cover of the annual knotweed (*Polygonum capitatum*). Ground-cover plants with a rather drier character include pirri-pirri-bur (*Acaena*), self-heal (*Prunella*), perhaps supplemented by the low-growing knotweed (*Polygonum affine*). Several plants in this group will be mentioned again in Chapter 3, under plants for drier soils.

The pretty stars of Polygonum affine *vary from white to deep pink.*

Leaves for contrast

Foliage plants can form a strong contrast against a background of fine-leaved plants. Such plants are notable for their leaves as well as their flowers. *Bergenia* is a good example. It has large,

12

shiny leaves which are attractive even in winter. They die back a little in the spring but then the flowers mean that the plant retains its attraction. Among the hostas there are also many beautiful species and cultivars which can be used for ground cover. The leaves vary in colour — green, grey-green, blue-green, and variegated. These plants deserve a place in every garden because of their lovely foliage. Apart from that, they often have flowers which are not unattractive although they do not last long. The various hostas are best combined with succulent ground-cover plants. If hostas are growing in full sun they need fairly damp soil. It is then not surprising that they are included among plants for half shade and the green-leaved ones for full shade.

The butterbur, *Petasites*, also has lovely, large, pale green leaves. It does not really belong in a very cultivated garden, but more in the woodland garden where it can grow beside water.

Always right There are some plants that are not fussy about the soil and can have a place in every border and every type of garden. The lady's mantle (*Alchemilla mollis*) is one such plant. The lovely, soft, green leaves, and the yellow-green flowers fit in almost anywhere, with the exception of very dry soils.

The various species and cultivars of cranesbill (*Geranium*),

Even if ground cover is rather bland, the effect can be livened up by contrasting foliage.

The beautiful, large leaves of Bergenia *provide a strong contrast.*

too, look equally good in a wild garden, in a woodland garden, and in a border as well as in a rockery. As well as having attractive foliage they often have pretty flowers so these cranesbills are certainly worth the effort of growing them.

A lovely border with lady's mantle, Alchemilla mollis, *in the foreground.*

In between Between the very low ground-cover plants and the foliage plants with a definite character, areas and small patches can be set with plants which are intermediate between these two groups as regards height and size of leaf. The 20cm (8in) high rock cress flowers early in the year and has grey leaves which give it a dry character. *Campanula* and *Heuchera* and the various *Potentilla* species are fairly neutral and can be combined with dry plants as well as the more succulent ones. The new cultivar of *Fragaria*, 'Pink Panda', fits in easily here. This new plant is not widely available and besides it is much more expensive compared with other perennials. That is because it comes under the Plant Variety Rights legislation and can only be sold by licensed retailers who pay a fee to the original breeder.

A splash of colour Most annuals flower abundantly during the summer and provide a splash of colour among the perennials. Perennials come up each year and in their main flowering season they flower either rather modestly or very freely. Sometimes they flower again later but always less intensively the second time. The advantage of annuals is that you can choose a different colour each year. If you have had a wonderful show of blue lobelia throughout the summer in between the other ground-cover plants, the following year you can choose from the beautiful shades of busy lizzies, or, when you want lively yellow or orange, nasturtiums, or the bright yellow and white *Limnanthes*. Plant the taller mignonette (*Reseda*) near the terrace so that you can enjoy the lovely scent of this plant. The flowers are certainly not striking, so it does not really belong in this section but it is worth mentioning among the other annuals.

Following page: During its flowering season Campanula poscharskyana *provides a lot of colour.*

Covering large areas

The shrubs and climbing plants mentioned in this section are suitable only for large areas. Of course that does not mean that you cannot plant the odd shrub or a few specimens between the perennial ground-cover plants, for example one of the many kinds of rose. The flowering quince (*Chaenomeles*), and the *Spiraea*, are both very suitable for this. These shrubs, especially the rose, flower abundantly over a long period and can therefore also be recommended for small gardens. The other shrubs and climbers that are mentioned are more suitable for slopes and large beds.

The sweet-scented Reseda odorata *is preferably planted by the terrace.*

Perennials	*Acaena, Alchemilla, Arabis, Bergenia, Campanula* (various species), *Cotula, Fragaria* 'Pink Panda', *Geranium* (various species), *Heuchera, Hosta* (various species and cultivars), *Lysimachia, Petasites, Polygonum, Potentilla, Prunella, Saxifraga, Trifolium, Veronica, Viola* (various species), several grasses.	*Left: Hostas are suitable for any type of garden. Here you see the slim, green-leafed* Hosta lancifolia.
Annuals	*Gazania, Impatiens, Limnanthes, Lobelia, Polygonum, Reseda, Sanvitalia, Silene, Tropaeolum, Viola.*	*Hostas, such as this variegated cultivar, are splendid foliage plants.*
Bulbs, tubers, and rhizomatous plants	*Anemone.*	
Shrubs and climbing plants	*Chaenomeles, Cotoneaster* (various species), *Hedera, Hydrangea, Lonicera, Parthenocissus,* roses (various cultivars), *Rubus* (several species), *Spiraea, Wisteria.*	

Plants for half shade

Most of the plants and shrubs mentioned here are discussed under sun lovers or shade plants. Half shade means that the area lies between sun and shade. Many plants that prefer a sunny position can also tolerate light shade and that is also of course the case with shade plants — plants that tolerate shade

can also be put in half shade. The variegated species and cultivars of several of them even prefer to grow in half shade, but their green-leafed relatives will tolerate more shade.

In the foreground the pirri-pirri-bur, Acaena, with the beautiful leaves of ivy, Hedera, in the background.

Perennials	*Acaena, Ajuga, Alchemilla, Asarum, Astilbe, Bergenia, Brunnera, Campanula* (various species), *Cotula, Dicentra, Duchesnea, Epimedium, Euphorbia, Fragaria, Galium, Geranium* (various species), *Glechoma, Heuchera, Hosta* (various species and cultivars), *Lamium, Lysimachia, Mazus, Mentha, Pachysandra, Petasites, Polygonum, Potentilla, Prunella, Pulmonaria, Saxifraga, Soleirolia, Tellima, Tiarella, Tolmiea, Trifolium, Veronica, Vinca, Viola* (various species), *Waldsteinia*, various ferns, several grasses.
Annuals	*Impatiens, Lobelia, Polygonum, Viola*.
Bulbs, tubers and rhizomatous plants	*Allium ursinum, Anemone* (various species), *Corydalis, Cyclamen, Eranthis, Polygonatum, Ranunculus*.
Shrubs and climbing plants	*Chaenomeles, Cotoneaster* (various species), *Hedera, Hydrangea, Hypericum, Lonicera, Mahonia, Parthenocissus, Rubus* (various species).

19

Shade-loving and shade-tolerant ground-cover plants

Plants need light in order to grow. It is therefore impossible to achieve a good, varied growth in deep shade. For example there is never a rich ground cover in a pine wood. Pine trees have dense foliage which excludes most of the light both winter and summer.

It is only where one or two trees have fallen so that light can reach the ground that a ground cover quickly springs up, apparently out of nothing. Along the woodland edge, too, where some sunlight can penetrate, a few ferns and mosses can be found, and between them some small plants have become established. If you do have places in the garden that receive hardly any light, it will be possible to grow something, even if only one of the many green-leafed species of ivy which even there will form a beautiful shiny surface.

Light but no direct sun

It is possible to have an interesting and varied ground cover in places which are light but out of the direct sun. Remember, however, that shade plants never flower very freely. You can achieve variety in the various shades of green and the differences in shape, size, and structure of the leaves.

Dark and shiny leaves

Apart from the ivy, the periwinkle, *Vinca* is a good ground-cover plant for shade. It is a vigorous grower, with dark green

The loveliest ground cover for large areas in shade is provided by the ivy. This one is Hedera helix *'Walthamensis.'*

leaves that are attractive even in winter. In spring the lovely flowers appear, blue, white, or mauve depending on the cultivar. *Vinca minor* is low growing, while *Vinca major* reaches twice the height. Asarabacca, *Asarum europaeum*, also has shiny, dark-green leaves which make a very attractive carpet.

The dark-green surface of the periwinkle, Vinca minor, *is enlivened by the lovely blue flowers of* Clematis x durandii.

Bright green and delicate flowers

It is nice to have some contrast in the part of the garden where there is little or no sun. You can plant something with bright green foliage between the two darker greens just mentioned. Try planting a few clumps of baby's tears, *Soleirolia soleirolii*, in the foreground or along the edge of a path or the terrace. These plants are often very cheap in the summer and, because given sufficient moisture they spread rapidly, you will need only a few of them to create an effect.

The white wood sorrel, *Oxalis acetosella*, is also low growing and has light-green leaves that contrast with the dark green of periwinkle and asarabacca. *Tiarella cordifolia* and *Tiarella wherryi* also provide good ground cover and form a carpet of light-green leaves that are softly hairy. They have pretty white flowers in spring. The rather larger leaves contrast well with dark-green foliage and delicate-leafed plants. *Tellima* and the pick-a-back plant, *Tolmiea*, have similar leaves to *Tiarella*.

TIP
Do not plant up dark places with variegated plants because these need more light than their green-leafed relatives.

21

Tellima grows to about 30cm (12in) high, *Tolmiea* about 40cm (16in). They go very well with periwinkle (*Vinca*), asarabacca (*Asarum*), bugle (*Ajuga*), ground ivy (*Glechoma*), and *Waldsteinia*, not only because of the contrasting colour of the foliage but because of the differences in height.

Spotted and striped

Variegated leaves can provide a nice contrast in shade. Lungwort, *Pulmonaria*, has fairly dull and often dark-green leaves, that in spite of their delicate markings and often pretty flowers make a rather sombre impression, particularly when the flowers are over. So plant them among and next to plants that are bright green. The deadnettle, *Lamium*, has various cultivars with prettily marked and variegated leaves. The most colourful of these come into their own alongside dark-green foliage. The delicately marked and spotted cultivars also look pretty next to light-green plants. When planting different groups, do consider the various heights. The prettily marked *Lamium* 'Hermann's Pride', and 'Silver Carpet' go well with the somewhat lower *Tiarella cordifolia*, with baby's tears or white wood sorrel.

Invasive plants

The invasive ground-cover plants are not so suitable for the small garden. These include the yellow-flowered strawberry,

Waldsteinia ternata *provides a colourful carpet when in flower.*

ground ivy, the variegated ground elder, and the variegated deadnettle. *Pachysandra*, too, is more suitable for large areas under trees and between shrubs.

Early flowering Plants that grow in shade often flower early in order to make the best use of light before the canopy closes over. That applies, for example, to barrenwort (*Epimedium*). For shade, choose the prettiest cultivars with white or yellow flowers and with a well-marked leaf, because dark leaves will not show up well. The beautiful bright-blue *Omphalodes* is worth a prominent place in half shade or shade merely on account of its flowers. The violet has quite small flowers so plant it where it will be noticed. It does not grow tall so it needs to be planted at the front of the border, along a path or between stepping stones, in combination with, for example, white clover. The yellow *Waldsteinia ternata* and the bugle, *Ajuga*, which can have blue, white or pink flowers, are also low growing. The much taller *Euphorbia amygdaloides*, and the variety *robbiae* are much taller. They flower from April to June. The variety can tolerate deep shade and because of its height, 60cm (24in), its greenish-yellow flowers, and its long, narrow dark-green leaves, it forms a nice contrast with low ground cover, for example *Tiarella*. London pride, *Saxifraga x urbium*, has very

A patch of light filters through from time to time onto the white flowers of Tiarella cordifolia.

T I P
Do not plant too many variegated kinds next to each other because it gives an untidy effect.

24

delicate flowers. Plant it against a dark background to show off the flowers to the best advantage.

Lungwort, Pulmonaria, *and* Waldsteinia *both flower in early spring.*

Ferns, special beauties for shade

When thinking about shade it is ferns that first spring to mind. Most of them have beautiful pinnate leaves and are bright green, so they provide a striking contrast with dark-leafed plants.

Unfortunately there are very few ferns suitable for ground cover. The bright-green ferns which provide ground cover include maidenhair fern (*Adiantum*), the beech fern (*Thelypteris phegopteris*) and the broad beech fern (*Phegopteris hexagonoptera*). The polypody (*Polypodium*) only has bright-green young shoots. The older leaves become very dark.

Other ferns for shade

You can plant a specimen plant or a group of ferns with light green foliage between the ground cover, such as the male fern (*Dryopteris filix-mas*), the hart's-tongue (*Phyllitis scolopendrium*), or one of the brilliant shield-ferns (*Polystichum*).

The hard-fern (*Blechnum spicant*) and the house holly-fern (*Cyrtomium falcatum*) can also have a place in the shade, but

Lamium galeobdolon *'Hermann's Pride' has beautifully marked leaves.*

they are less striking because they have dark-green leaves. Set them against light-green ground cover.

Grasses for shade *Carex plantaginea*, which is actually a sedge, is a beautiful plant for the shade with broad leaves and delicate, brown flowers. Among the woodrushes, too, there are several nice species that can be used as ground cover, but they are seen to best advantage only when they are planted in small groups and patches among very low ground cover.

Ground-cover plants for shade with other plants When the ground-cover plants form patches under a group of shrubs there will be scarcely any need to add other plants here too. A large area, however, with ground cover of more or less the same height can be rather monotonous. The effect can be livened up by planting a few groups or one or two single specimens of taller plants.

Polypody, Polypodium vulgare, *is satisfied with a dry situation*

Among the good shade-loving plants that can be used in this way are, apart from the ferns, several species and cultivars of *Rogersia*, Solomon's seal (*Polygonatum nudiflorum*), and the bamboo *Sasa veitchii*.

Perennials *Ajuga, Asarum, Duchesnea, Epimedium, Euphorbia, Glechoma, Hosta* (various species and cultivars), *Lamium,*

Carex plantaginea *is a beautiful sedge that can tolerate a fair amount of shade.*

Omphalodes, Pachysandra, Pulmonaria, Saxifraga, Solei-rolia, Tellima, Tiarella, Tolmiea, Vinca, Viola, Waldsteinia, various ferns, several grasses.

Bulbs, tubers and rhizomatous plants   *Ranunculus.*

Shrubs and climbing plants   *Hedera, Hydrangea.*

Rodgersia podophylla 'Rotlaub' makes a beautiful specimen plant but can also be planted in a group as taller ground cover.

Plant combinations for sandy soil

Sandy soils, which contain little or no humus, are often dry, because there is nothing to hold the water. They are also very low in plant nutrients.

*Opposite page:
The central strip
between two sections
of a drive can be made
especially attractive
by planting with all
kinds of Sedum and
Sempervivum species.
The grey-leafed
Festuca provides a
nice contrast.*

If you want to be able to grow a wide variety of plants, without being dependent on the limited selection that will grow on very poor soil, then soil improvement is unavoidable. It will be necessary to dig the soil well and work compost and possibly peat or manure into the lowest layers. Unfortunately you cannot do this once and for all. After a time, perhaps as early as the following year, depending on how much compost and manure has been added, you will need to apply compost and manure between the plants. If you want to enjoy the great variety of plants which flower luxuriantly, you will have to continue improving the soil. If you do not, the soil will gradually deteriorate and become poor and sandy once more.

Sun lovers

There are plenty of sun lovers for sandy soil. You can achieve a design with grey-leafed plants, interspersed with smaller or larger groups of taller perennials and a single shrub. Because the grey-leafed plants predominate they are used as a basis, with suggestions for plants which can be combined with them.

Grey with white and yellow

You can begin with the grey-leafed plants which go well with yellow and white flowers and plants that combine with these. Yarrow (*Achillea chrysocoma*), pearl everlasting (*Anaphalis*), mouse ear (*Cerastium*), *Raoulia*, catchfly (*Silene uniflora*

*The pirri-pirri-bur is
particularly nice when
the prickly seeds form.
This is the red* Acaena
microphylla *'Copper
Carpet.'*

T I P

Apart from variation in foliage and in flowering habit, remember to consider flowering season so as to have a spread of blooms through the year.

29

'Robin Whitebreast')and the bunnies' ears (*Stachys byzantina* 'Silver Carpet') all have grey leaves and either white, yellow or inconspicuous flowers. When you are combining these plants be careful to consider the height and the size of the leaf because some of them differ too little to make an interesting ground cover. If they are planted alongside each other the effect will be rather messy and unclear. *Raoulia* and bunnies' ears form the two extremes of this series. The former has a very low growth habit and minute leaves, the latter has pretty, distinctive leaves. The silver-leaved species of the pirri-pirri-bur, for example *Acaena buchannii* and *Acaena magellanica*, form pretty, vigorous ground cover. Add a few groups of grey-leaved grasses for their contrasting shape to make an interesting picture. The ground-covering *Festuca glauca* and *Koeleria glauca* are especially suitable, to which can be added the tall, also grey-leafed blue oat grass *Helictotrichon sempervirens*, for a striking feature. *Gypsophila*, with its delicate flowers, can best be placed next to a plant which has a strong leaf structure, for example *Geranium renardii*. For a taller feature among the grey-leafed ground cover you can choose one of the beautiful cultivars of the common German flag, *Iris germanica*. The tall, sword-shaped leaves which are grey-green, stand out very well here. The *Yucca* has a similar

The pale-yellow pearl everlasting, Anaphalis triplinervis, *looks lovely among other grey-leafed plants, or, as here, with the red-leafed plantain.*

structure, forming a stout clump of leaves with tall sprays of white flowers. Finally there are the tall mulleins, especially *Verbascum bombyciferum*, with splendid rosettes of grey, felty leaves and yellow flowers like huge torches that can easily reach 1.5m (5ft), a real must.

Annuals that deserve a place in this predominantly grey planting include *Gazania pinnata* with yellow flowers, and the white *Senecio cineraria*.

The interplay of the greenish-yellow Euphorbia cyparissias, *and a pale blue self-heal.*

Grey with pink, rose red, and blue

It is amazing that most of the grey-leafed plants have white or yellow flowers — sunshine colours. In a grey planting scheme with pink, lilac, and blue flowering plants the grey woolly thymes make a lovely, low ground cover. The taller bunnies' ears can be put in here with the yellow-flowered planting, and irises, but in pinks, blues, and mauves. Blue-grey grasses, *Gypsophila*, and the white *Senecio* can be added to this. The cat's ear, *Antennaria dioica*, with its pink flowers, remains quite low-growing. Put this little plant in a prominent position or the flowers will probably be overlooked. Keep an eye on it too, because it could be choked by more vigorous plants. A rock garden is really the best place for the cat's ear. Among the rock roses, *Helianthemum*, with its small grey-green leaves, there are cultivars with yellow or white flowers and at the same

Two contrasting grey leaves; the pirri-pirri-bur, Acaena magellanica, *and the bunnies' ears,* Stachys byzantina.

31

time some pretty red and pink ones. A very attractive, low-growing plant is the self-heal, *Prunella*, with pink, blue, mauve, and crimson cultivars. They fit in extremely well among the grey leaves. The cultivars of the very early-flowering alpine phlox, *Phlox subulata*, and the edging plant *Arabis*, are not out of place here. The blue-flowering, grey-leafed catmint, *Nepeta*, and the pink cultivars of *Arabis* make a good transition between high and low. Several perennials which provide a taller feature in this scheme are, for instance, the mallow, *Malva moschata*, several thistles, such as *Echinops* and *Eryngium*, but also the perennial *Salvia* and marjoram, *Origanum*, with some cultivars that are not used as culinary herbs but as ornamental plants in the border. A good annual that deserves a place in this planting is the lovely *Brachycome*, with blue flowers that look like small daisies. *Erigeron karvinskianus* looks very like it but has pink and white flowers. If the winter is not too wet and cold this little plant will self-seed very well.

Green leaves Besides the many grey-leafed plants there are also greener plants which are suitable for a sunny spot on sandy soil. You can, of course, plant a mixture of all sorts of colours and shades next to each other, but below there are a few suggestions for

A planting scheme in pink and grey with large areas of different self-heals, Prunella vulgaris.

colour combinations which lie close together in the spectrum. The yellow bird's-foot trefoil (*Lotus corniculatus*), the pale orange *Potentilla x tonguei*, and the biting stonecrop (*Sedum acre*) all deserve a mention in a bright planting scheme of orange and yellow shades. The rather taller evening primrose (*Oenothera missouriensis*) forms a colourful yellow display which is very striking in the flowering season. The various species of broom with their particular growth habit provide a nice change among the other plants. The bright orange hawkweeds, *Hieracium*, make a striking feature, although because of their rosette of leaves they need to be grown among very low ground cover, for example stonecrop. The hawkweed can also be planted to cover larger areas. The chamomile (*Chamaemelum nobile* 'Treneague'), and the rupturewort (*Herniaria*) have no flowers or very few and are attractive alternatives to grass only because of their bright green leaves. The pearlwort too, *Sagina subulata*, forms a nice carpet in place of grass. It has tiny, white flowers that could look good among ground cover with flowers in shades of blue, pink or red. For a lovely contrast you can plant a big patch of thrift, *Armeria maritima*, which has pink flowers, or the blue bellflower, *Campanula carpatica*. *Ceratostigma*, with its dark green leaves which turn colour in the autumn, and its gentian-

Biting stonecrop, Sedum acre, *and the creeping willow,* Salix repens.

The low-growing soapwort, Saponaria ocymoides, *flowers in early spring.*

blue flowers, looks nice here. The choice among the cranes-bills, *Geranium*, is so wide that it is possible to find one for any situation.

In the sun and on poor soil you can cover large areas with the white-flowered *Geranium cantabrigiense* 'Biokovo' which will also grow in half shade, the deep purple *Geranium dalmaticum* with the beautiful leaf which turns colour, the magenta *Geranium sanguineum* and its white-flowered cultivar 'Album.' *Geranium cinereum* with its various cultivars and varieties is also suitable for these situations.

The pearlwort, Sagina subulata, *will certainly make a lovely carpet while it is in flower.*

Perennials *Acaena, Achillea, Anaphalis, Antennaria, Arabis, Armeria, Aubrieta, Campanula* (some species), *Cerastium, Ceratostigma, Chamaemelum, Dianthus, Euphorbia, Geranium,* (some species), *Gysophila, Helianthemum, Herniaria, Hieracium, Lithodora, Lotus, Nepeta, Oenothera, Origanum, Phlox, Potentilla, Prunella, Raoulia, Sagina, Saponaria, Saxifraga, Sedum* (some species), *Sempervivum, Silene, Stachys, Thymus* (some species), a few grasses including *Festuca, Koeleria,* and *Phalaris.*

Annuals *Brachycome, Dorotheanthus, Erigeron, Gazania, Lobularia, Reseda, Senecio, Silene, Tropaeolum.*

TIP

Plant early-flowering varieties near the house or beside a path which is used regularly. That will mean maximum enjoyment.

Bulbs, tubers and rhizomatous plants	*Oxalis.*
Shrubs and climbing plants	*Berberis, Calluna, Cotoneaster, Cytisus, Rubus, Salix* (creeping willow).

Geranium cantabrigiense 'Biokovo' is useful ground cover in half shade.

In half shade   Half shade is the transition area between full sun and shade. There are, of course, gradations within it. In the shade there is virtually no sun but there is light. Full sun can be defined as the area where there is at least six hours direct sunlight each day, assuming there is no cloud cover.

The area in between receives direct sunlight for between two and five hours a day. In light shade, which has five hours sun each day, the list of plants includes both those which are on the list of sun lovers as well as those for half shade such as bellflowers (*Campanula portenschlagiana* and *C.poscharskyana*), chamomile (*Chamaemelum*), rupturewort (*Herniaria*), hawkweed (*Hieracium*), self-heal (*Prunella*), pearlwort (*Sagina*), grasses, and a few *Geranium* species, although some of them will also be satisfied with less sun. That is really the whole list, which shows that on dry ground shade is a big problem. The plants given in that list can of course also be grown in half shade and many of them are at their best there.

Perennials	*Astilbe chinensis*, *Campanula* (some species), *Chamaemelum*, *Doronicum*, *Geranium* (some species), *Herniaria*, *Hieracium*, *Prunella*, *Sagina*, *Saxifraga*, *Sedum* (some species), *Vinca*, grasses such as *Festuca*.
Annuals	*Silene*.
Shrubs and climbing plants	*Calluna*, *Cotoneaster*, *Rubus*, *Salix*.

All kinds of low-growing plants, including thymes, cranesbills, and soapworts, form their own communities between stepping stones.

In the shade Shade plants generally like rather damp soil with plenty of humus. The list of shade tolerant plants for sandy soil is therefore rather limited. It is a good idea to improve the soil and make sure that plenty of humus is added to help retain sufficient moisture.

Right: Pachysandra is particularly suitable for covering large areas.

Ferns Fortunately there are some ferns which will do reasonably well and sometimes even very well on poor soil. Bracken, *Pteridium aquilinum*, is very invasive when the conditions suit it. It makes a lovely "wood" with its majestic, upright growth. In the spring it is lovely to see how the bright-green growth unfolds, and in the autumn it is astonishing how the foliage changes from golden-yellow to a rich chestnut brown.

It is a pretty fern, especially under tall trees, but it should never be planted. If you already have it, it can be combined with other vigorous plants such as ivy, rose of Sharon (*Hypericum calycinum*), *Pachysandra* and the variegated deadnettle (*Lamium*). Polypody (*Polypodium vulgare* and *P. interjectum*), and the beech fern (*Thelypteris phegopteris*), come into a very different category. They grow much lower and spread much less. They go best with plants which are not very tall and also do not have a thick root mat and a vigorous growth, such as wood sorrel (*Oxalis acetosella*), sweet violet (*Viola odorata*), and the lovely, white-flowered wood anemone (*Anemone nemorosa*) and its cultivars.

One of the nicest little plants for early spring: the scented sweet violet, Viola odorata.

From small and delicate to tall and strong

The woodland character which is suggested by the ferns can be emphasized with large patches of woodruff, *Galium odoratum*. This little plant with delicate, needle-like leaves, needs ground cover alongside it with larger leaves to provide a contrast. Comfrey, *Symphytum grandiflorum*, is one such plant. The leaves of lily-of-the-valley, *Convallaria majalis*, also provide a lovely green carpet, and in May the delicate, white, scented flowers make an absolute picture. You can try planting a few clumps of the strong-smelling ramsons, *Allium ursinum*, or of the bluebell, *Hyacinthoides non-scripta*,

Opposite page: The bellflower, Campanula portenschlagiana, *is very free flowering.*

which flowers profusely in the spring with deep blue flowers on fine stems. There are more details about this in Chapter 5, under woodland. *Geranium nodosum* is one of the few cranesbills that will still grow well in shade in poor, sandy soil. The value of this cranesbill lies in its shiny, light-green leaves which form a pretty carpet.

It never flowers vigorously, but the lilac-pink flowers appear at intervals throughout the summer. The plant spreads by means of underground runners, and also seeds freely. It does spread quite easily so that in a limited area the young plants need to be removed regularly.

A ground cover of woodruff, Galium odoratum, *with the ostrich fern,* Matteuccia struthiopteris, *and the blue* Centaurea montana.

Perennials   *Galium, Geranium* (some species), *Lamium, Oxalis acetosella, Pachysandra, Symphytum, Viola.*

Ferns   *Thegopteris connectilis, Polypodium vulgare, Pteridium aquilinum.*

Bulbs, tubers, and rhizomatous plants   *Anemone, Convallaria.*

Shrubs and climbing plants   *Hedera, Hypericum.*

Plant combinations for clay soil

Heavy clay is the most difficult of all soils to work. It is often very fertile and contains lime, but in wet weather the soil becomes sticky and compacts easily because the particles are very small, and in dry weather it becomes rock-hard and often cracks.

The big problem with clay soil is its structure, which needs to be made more loose so that surplus water can drain away, and at the same time to let more air into the soil. It is also important that the soil should hold more water in dry periods. For improving this kind of soil it is recommended that sand and peat or peat dust be worked into the lower layer (from 50 to 60cm — 20 to 24in). If you do this in the winter and leave the ground roughly dug over until the spring, the frost will help to break down the soil. Determine if there is an impenetrable layer of clay. In that case it is often not enough to work just the top 60cm (24in), because this clay layer will hold the water and there will still be enormous puddles on the surface despite all your hard work. The following list of plants assumes that the soil has been improved.

This low-growing lady's mantle, Alchemilla alpina, *has a silver edge to the leaf which gives an interesting effect. Opposite page: One of the loveliest of the white-flowered cultivars,* Epimedium x youngianum 'Niveum.'

Sun lovers   Fortunately there is a wide choice of ground cover for clay soil. If you have clay soil in your garden you have one big advantage — roses will grow tremendously well there. It is not for nothing that you find many rose-growers in areas of clay soil in, say, East Anglia.

Pirri-pirri-burs and other low growers   For large beds the pirri-pirri-bur, *Acaena*, is an outstanding ground-cover plant, which when it likes the conditions, can be

TIP

On wet ground it is advisable to plant in spring, because a lot of rain, together with frost, will do your young plants no good at all.

41

very invasive. There is a good selection, with a wide choice of leaf colour. When you have chosen a grey-leafed *Acaena* as ground cover it is nice to plant a contrast here and there such as the bearded iris. The foliage of the *Iris germanica* hybrids is often still attractive in winter. Besides this, iris has flowers in lovely colours and delicate shades in May and June. *Ceratostigma plumbaginoides* goes well with it, particularly since the leaf turns colour in autumn, and of course on account of the bright-blue flowers. Other low-growing plants that do well on clay are chamomile, *Chamaemelum*, and *Cotula*. If lady's mantle is mentioned you immediately think of *Alchemilla mollis*, which reaches 40 to 60cm (16 to 24in) and is used in flower arranging. There are, however, some very low-growing species, such as *Alchemilla alpina*, *Alchemilla erythropoda*, and *Alchemilla vulgaris*. These go well with plants like *Campanula glomerata*, *C. carpatica*, *Phuopsis*, and the rather taller species of skullcap, *Scutellaria*. Plant a group of Japanese anemones to give variety — these grow particularly well on clay and spread freely. If this plant was not so attractive you would almost call it a weed.

Cranesbills and storksbills There are various storksbills, of which *Erodium x variabile* and its cultivars grow no higher than 10cm (4in) including

The bellflower, Campanula glomerata, has very bright purple flowers, which is a reason for not planting large beds of it.

flowers. There are also other, taller, storksbills but for those you need to go to a nursery which has a particular stock. The annual RHS publication *Plant Finder* lists the availability of particular plants. The cranesbill, *Geranium*, is closely related to the storksbill. There are many different low-growing species which will make an attractive carpet on clay. They are the ones suitable for the rock garden, such as *Geranium dalmaticum*, *G. cinerium* and *G. sanguinium*, together with their cultivars.

Rosa '*Snow Carpet*' and '*Pink Drift*' make good ground cover.

Perennials *Acaena* (some species), *Alchemilla, Anemone, Campanula* (some species), *Ceratostigma, Chamaemelum, Corydalis, Cotula, Erodium, Euphorbia, Fragaria, Geranium* (some species), *Helianthemum, Mentha, Petasites, Phuopsis, Potentilla, Scutellaria, Trifolium, Viola*, bamboo (some species).

Shrubs *Chaenomeles* (some species), *Cotoneaster* (some species), *Rosa*.

Acaena anserinifolia is a lush, green pirri-pirri-bur.

In half shade The choice of plants for half shade is wider than for sunny areas. You can create lovely carpets, with nice contrasts in leaf shape and flower colour, although flowering is less profuse in half shade and shade.

The earliest flowers

The first flowers in spring are always especially welcome. In half shade those include *Brunnera macrophylla* and *Omphalodes verna*, with blue or white flowers. These look rather like forget-me-nots. *Brunnera* has larger leaves so it contrasts well with small- and delicate-leafed plants, such as woodruff, *Galium odoratum*. The butterbur flowers early, even in February if the weather is mild. The wild *Petasites hybridus* has lilac-pink flowers, while the smaller and less invasive *Petasites albus* is white. The latter is more suitable for the garden not only because it is less vigorous but because it is shorter and has smaller leaves. This is rather like the *Brunnera* leaf, although that of the butterbur is a brighter green. Lungwort, *Pulmonaria*, has white, pink, red, or blue flowers in April and May. The leaves are long and finely marked. Another early plant is *Euphorbia amygdaloides*, and the variety *robbiae*.

The latter in particular can tolerate quite deep shade and also a fair amount of drought. Plant lily-of-the-valley for a delicious scent in May.

All these plants have quite large leaves and grow to between 15 and 60cm (6 and 24in). It is nice to combine them with ground cover. This makes for an interesting effect.

A lovely combination: the blue Brunnera *with the beautiful, soft-pink tree peony, photographed in the famous garden of Sissinghurst Castle, Kent, England.*

Low for contrast The leaves of woodruff, *Galium odoratum*, are still bright green in the spring. The plant provides lighter patches, especially with its white flowers, among darker foliage. Bugle, *Ajuga*, is also low growing, with dark green, purple-green or variegated leaves. Make use of these nice contrasts in planting schemes.

Do not put dark green next to dark green, or two different variegated plants side by side. The same applies to the deadnettle as to the bugle, because both have cultivars with leaves which are strongly marked or coloured.

The bright-green, fern-like foliage of the corydalis, *Corydalis lutea* and *Corydalis ochroleuca*, look lovely against a background of dark-leafed bugle, wild ginger (*Asarum*), or lily-of-the-valley (*Convallaria majalis*). Apart from the variegated leaves of bugle (*Ajuga*), and deadnettle (*Lamium*), the variegated clover, *Trifolium repens* 'Quinquefolium', is also suitable for planting in light shade on clay. This little plant has a leaf which is so subtly coloured that it scarcely appears to be variegated at all — reddish brown, with a delicate, green edge. Plant the anemones, *Anemone sylvestris*, and *Anemone aconitifolium* (*Ranunculus aconitifolius*), preferably in combination with dark foliage, such as wild ginger (*Asarum*)

The massive leaves of the butterbur, Petasites hybridus.

Left: The beautifully marked leaves of Trifolium repens *'Quinquefolium.'*

and periwinkle (*Vinca*). From time to time when making a planting plan for the garden it is important that some quite large, definite areas are planted with one species. The size of the area in question will naturally depend on the size of the garden.

The fern-like foliage and the creamy-yellow flowers of Corydalis ochroleuca.

For large beds For a planting scheme like that it is preferable to choose plants with a clear leaf shape, such as butterbur (*Petasites*), *Brunnera*, or *Omphalodes*. Lady's mantle (*Alchemilla mollis*), too, *Tellima*, and its relative the pick-a-back plant deserve a mention here. The wild strawberry does not have a very noticeable leaf, but it needs the space because it grows very vigorously. The shrubs listed below also demand a large area either because they are very vigorous or because of their growth habit.

Perennials *Ajuga, Alchemilla, Anemone, Asarum, Brunnera, Chamaemelum, Convallaria, Corydalis, Cotula, Epimedium, Euphorbia, Fragaria, Galium, Geranium* (some species), *Heuchera, Houttuynia, Lamium, Mentha, Omphalodes, Petasites, Phuopsis, Pulmonaria, Tellima, Tolmiea, Trifolium, Viola.*

Shrubs *Chaenomeles* (some species), *Cotoneaster* (some species), *Hypericum, Rubus* (some species).

In the shade   Most of the plants in the following list have already been discussed under plants for half shade, except for the *Epimedium* and the *Houttuynia*. *Epimedium* is fairly neutral and can be planted either in small groups among low ground cover, or as a large area between other ground-cover plants. It is easy to combine with other plants, preferably woodland ones. *Houttuynia* demands more space, because if it likes the conditions it grows very rapidly. For a dark corner, with other variegated plants nearby, *Houttuynia cordata* 'Chameleon' gives a splash of colour. In large groups it looks right only where there is a lot of space and the other groups of plants are also on a large scale.

Perennials   *Ajuga, Asarum, Epimedium, Euphorbia, Houttuynia, Lamium, Omphalodes, Pulmonaria, Tellima, Tolmiea, Viola.*

This cultivar of Houttuynia cordata *is called 'Chameleon.'*

Woodland, heaths, and wet soil

It is often very dry under trees and shrubs because they take a lot of moisture out of the soil, but on the other hand, the annual leaf fall adds humus to the soil which helps to hold moisture.

The spring-flowering cowslip, Primula veris.

Growth under trees and shrubs

After heavy rain the soil beneath trees is wet, but it can dry out during a long sunny spell. The leaf canopy shades the ground from the sun so it can be assumed that the soil is humus-rich, fertile, and somewhat damp. Most plants which were mentioned in Chapter 2 (plants for normal garden soil in shade and half shade) are often suitable here. In a woodland garden cultivated varieties are avoided in order to give the planting as natural a look as possible. Various species of plants are encountered in similar situations in the wild.

Low and delicate

Under trees a carpet can be made up of all kinds of delicate, soft-hued little plants, which together make lovely ground cover. The white wood sorrel, *Oxalis acetosella*, has already been mentioned. The pale-lilac *Corydalis solida* provides some colour in the spring, together with the sweet violet, *Viola odorata*. The delicate May lily, *Maianthemum bifolium*, must have space, otherwise it is soon overgrown by other plants and becomes overlooked. It is not a problem if some bare ground is left around this plant. Perhaps the open area will acquire a covering of moss, which will look pretty.

The cornel has one species which is a perennial, *Cornus canadensis* — a very pretty, creeping plant with small white flowers above a star of leaves. Some forms produce red fruits.

This plant is not very obtrusive, which is why it is mentioned in this list. Another particularly nice plant that needs space and attention because it is slow-growing is the *Hepatica*. Some plants of the pale-yellow primrose, *Primula vulgaris*, or the cowslip, *Primula veris*, are at home here, like ransoms, *Allium ursinum*, that has pretty, white flowers and smells of onions. To make a taller feature in this low ground cover plant some clumps of cuckoo pint, *Arum italicum* or *Arum maculatum*, together with some attractive ferns. The dwarf cyclamens must not have too much competition, because otherwise they get trampled on, which is a shame for such an attractive little plant. Species such as the autumn-flowering *Cyclamen hederafolium* and *C. purpurascens* have a place at the edge of a path or around the base of a tall tree.

Pretty for a time Unfortunately most bulbs, tubers, and rhizomatous plants are attractive for only a short time. The foliage dies back after flowering and there is just bare ground left. It is a good thing to plant these where a bare area in summer does not matter. Ransoms (*Allium ursinum*), wood anemone (*Anemone nemorosa*), the yellow *Anemone ranunculoides*, *Corydalis solida*, celandine *(Ranunculus ficaria)*, the pretty weed with brilliant yellow flowers, and the winter aconite (*Eranthis*) all flower in

Cornus canadensis forms a nice clump between various hostas.

The celandine,
Ranunculus ficaria,
dies back after
flowering.

early spring and then fade quickly. You can plant here some clumps of Spanish bluebell, *Hyacinthoides hispanica* (syn. *Scilla hispanica* and *S. campanulata*, the older more familiar names), and the bluebell, *Hyacynthoides non-scripta* (syn. *Scilla non-scripta*), in between. These mainly blue-flowered bulbs form a carpet of colour under trees and among shrubs in the spring. The bluebell is very common indeed in Great Britain, although in the west of Scotland it is a plant of hedgerows and open grassland. There are also perennials which lose their leaves or become rather ugly after flowering. The leopard's bane, *Doronicum*, for example, has brilliant yellow flowers above bright-green leaves in the spring. It does, however, lose its freshness after flowering, especially in dry places. *Hylomecon japonicum* with its flowers like poppies is also a plant that dies off after flowering but it is very attractive in its season and is therefore worth the effort.

Restful areas
Between places with rather small-scale planting (such as that described under "low and delicate") it is good to create a few areas which are more restful. These can consist of large expanses of just one species. If that is too big an area, then it is nice to add a feature of a single group or just a few specimens of a plant that makes a definite contrast with the ground cover.

The blue Spanish hyacinth, Hyacinthoides hispanica, *and the white woodruff,* Galium odoratum.

Ferns can be used, but also butterbur, *Petasites*, with its large leaves, and Solomon's seal, *Polygonatum*. The tall, biennial foxglove, *Digitalis purpurea*, with its strong vertical growth, is at home in places in the woodland where the sun regularly penetrates the tree canopy. This plant helps to break up an otherwise rather flat planting.

Plants which are suitable for low, restful areas include bugle (*Ajuga reptans*), wild ginger (*Asarum*), lily-of-the-valley (*Convallaria*), the sub-shrub *Gaultheria procumbens*, water avens (*Geum rivale*), and periwinkle (*Vinca*). The white anemones, *Anemone sylvestris* and *Anemone aconitifolium*, look very delicate with their thin stems, but make no mistake, these lovely little plants will soon make a very attractive carpet with pretty, deeply-incised leaves above which the white flowers show up very well. Although these anemones are woodland plants they will not thrive in deep shade.

The shiny leaf of the asarabacca, Asarum europaeum, *contrasts beautifully with the ferns.*

Rough places and large beds

Invasive plants and very vigorous climbing plants which include the large-leafed ivies, honeysuckle (*Lonicera*), and various species and cultivars of bramble (*Rubus*), only have a place among shrubs and under trees if space permits. The vigorous climbers are best grown under trees or in between large, fully grown shrubs. They must be kept in check among

In the wild, bugle, Ajuga, *grows in open places in woodland.*

51

newly planted shrubs, because they will otherwise smother them or stunt their growth.

Small-leaved varieties of ivy, which are less vigorous, are often appropriate under shrubs, as is the evergreen ground-covering *Euonymus fortunei* — the cultivar 'Minimus', which has small, dark leaves, is particularly suitable for small beds.

Ground-cover perennials which quickly cover large areas must not be planted under very low-growing shrubs or the latter will soon be overwhelmed and all you will see is a mound of perennials.

Wild strawberry, *Fragaria vesca*, and the variegated deadnettle, *Lamium galeobdolon*, are two examples. Wood-ruff, *Galium odoratum*, and the deadnettle, *Lamium maculatum*, are less aggressive. Bistort, *Polygonum bistorta*, is very pretty and deserves planting in a small group on the edge of the wood. Perhaps there is a damp place or a small pond where it can grow. It looks very attractive when the flowers are reflected in water.

More cultivated

In woodland areas and shrub borders it is sometimes nice not to have just wild plants, but to plant here and there a bed or a clump of a more cultivated species or even a special cultivar. Hostas are a good example — they are beautiful foliage plants.

The flowers of the evergreen Euonymus fortunei *'Dart's Cardinal.'*

The green-leafed cultivars in particular fit into natural surroundings. The variegated cultivars, like all plants which result from the crossing of two or more species, look much more "cultivated." These are more suitable for the transition between the wild woodland garden and the rather more colourful planting in a border. In this transition area there is also a place for *x Heucherella*, and the closely related *Tellima* and *Tiarella*.

Although lungwort, *Pulmonaria officinale*, does occur sporadically in the wild, it should be planted towards the more cultivated end of the woodland garden. This lungwort is not grown very frequently, in contrast to the various cultivars which are often variegated and flower early in the year with small white, blue, or pink flowers. Unfortunately the plant is not very exciting after its flowering season, especially the green-leafed one, so it is a good idea to plant it where it will not attract attention during the summer.

The leaves of the yellow-flowered comfrey, *Symphytum grandiflorum*, look not unlike the lungwort and they are rather boring. The plant is pretty on account of the flowers. London pride is lovely. This low-growing plant forms rosettes of shiny leaves that are evergreen. The delicate flowers look like a white cloud above the rosette. There is also a variegated cultivar but

A woodland path with wild ginger, Asarum caudatum. *In the background a group of hostas.*

Following page:
The low comfrey, Symphytum grandiflorum, *with the lovely ostrich fern,* Matteuccia struthiopteris.

53

this is not so attractive and looks rather sickly. *Omphalodes*, too, needs to be planted in a relatively large bed. The leaves are attractive and give a restful picture in a delicate-leafed planting of, for example, woodruff, *Galium odoratum*. *Omphalodes* has very attractive blue flowers similar to forget-me-nots. The white cultivar is also pretty but less noticeable than the blue. Deadnettle, *Lamium*, can be planted in the wild garden as well as in the more cultivated parts. It depends very much on the species and the cultivars. You need to keep in mind that the cultivars with three-coloured leaves are the least strong and need the most light. These do not, therefore, belong in the wild woodland garden.

Omphalodes verna *appears to flow like a stream between the pine trees.*

Perennials *Ajuga, Anemone, Asarum, Convallaria, Cornus canadensis, Corydalis, Doronicum, Epimedium, Fragaria, Galium, Geum, x Heucherella, Hosta, Hylomecon, Lamium, Maianthemum, Omphalodes, Oxalis, Petasites, Polygonatum, Polygonum, Pulmonaria, Saxifraga, Symphytum, Tellima, Tiarella, Vinca, Viola odorata*, all the ferns mentioned in this book.

Bulbs, tubers, and rhizomatous plants *Allium, Anemone, (A. nemorosa* and *A. ranunculoides), Corydalis (C. solida* and *C. bulbosa), Cyclamen, Ranunculus.*

Shrubs and climbing plants   *Hedera* (various species and cultivars), *Euonymus fortunei* and its cultivars, *Gaultheria, Lonicera* (species and cultivars), *Rubus* (some species and cultivars), *Vaccinium*.

One of the lovely winter-flowering cultivars of the alpine heath, Erica carnea *'December Red.'*

Heaths   Many low-growing and creeping species and cultivars among the heathland plants are discussed in this book because of their ground-covering characteristics. There are, however, so many large and specific families of plants that it is impossible to talk about them all. The heaths, the *Ericaceae*, like acid soil. So you cannot just plant a heath or heather garden in any garden without first of all determining the pH (acidity) of the soil. Heaths are at home on acid sandy or peaty soils. The cross-leaved heath, *Erica tetralix*, occurs in the wild in bogs and on wet peaty soils.

Furthermore a heather garden does not look right in every situation. To have a heather garden in the middle of a flat field looks odd and is certainly not appropriate. Have a look at natural heather and heath areas in the wild and decide whether the plants will look right in your garden. Many people think that a heather garden needs little or no maintenance. This is just not true. If you want to be sure of a colourful display of heathers and heaths you need to clip them regularly and, if necessary, correct the pH of the soil. The heaths of, for example, the Breckland in East Anglia, which is on Greensand, seem to be growing on very poor, sandy soil, but the presence of some organic material and the correct pH mean that plants such as *Calluna* can be grown there successfully. These soils also contain various fungi with which the heathers have a symbiotic relationship.

Many heathlands are grazed by sheep or cattle which provide cheap "mowing machines." If this is not done and nature is allowed to take its course the heath will eventually disappear and be replaced by coarse grasses, brambles, elderberry, and other plants that find the conditions to their liking. Regular clipping is therefore a very important factor in a heather garden.

If you do want to plant a heather garden you can choose plants from the various species of *Erica* — the heaths, and *Calluna* — heather. As a shrub plant use, for example, the lovely Juneberry (*Amelanchier*), or one of the attractive species of pine tree. There are some which have a low, spreading growth form but also some that become large trees. The juniper, *Juniperus communis*, belongs in a heather garden, too, and if you choose a cultivar with a strong, pillar-like shape it can provide a vertical element.

Perennials *Antennaria, Festuca glauca, Koeleria glauca.*

Mineral soil *Arctostaphyllus uva-ursi, Calluna vulgaris* and its many cultivars, *Cytisus* (some species), *Genista* (some species), *Salix repens, Ulex.*

Conifers *Juniperus* (some species and cultivars), *Microbiota, Taxus* (some species and cultivars).

Peat soil *Empetrum, Erica* (many species and the cultivars), *Gaultheria procumbens, Vaccinium vitis-idaea.*

Damp to wet soils In peat areas in places such as Wales and the west of Scotland which have high rainfall you will come across damp to wet ground with a lot of surface water in the form of attractive pools. But low-lying areas beside rivers are often waterlogged and have their own specific plant communities. In the garden lower-lying areas can often be damp and the edges of a pond also need the planting to be adapted for the same reason.

Sun lovers *Hydrocotyle nova-zealandiae* can be successfully grown under azaleas and in low areas where there is regularly standing water. It is a small, attractive, plant with round, shiny

Opposite page: The early-flowering butterbur with the small leaves, Petasites albus.

leaves that makes a nice ground layer with the marsh fern, *Thelypteris palustris*, as a contrast. Colour can be provided by the yellow creeping jenny, among which some clumps of other marsh plants can be set, to give some variation in height. On wet ground this could be the marsh marigold, *Caltha palustris*, and also some species of *Iris* which give a contrast with their grass-like leaves. The butterbur can be put in places where its invasive nature will not cause problems to surrounding plants. *Petasites album* is less aggressive and has lovely, soft-green leaves, which only develop after the cream-coloured flowers. The sturdy and free-flowering bistort, *Polygonum bistorta*, can be recommended in combination with butterbur.

Sun *Hydrocotyle, Lysimachia, Petasites, Polygonum, Thelypteris palustris*, grasses, including *Carex* and *Luzula*.

Half shade Some plants which were described under the woodland garden or for planting in half shade in normal garden soil are also suitable for the damp to wet soils. The only ground-cover plant that has not so far been mentioned is the low *Gunnera magellanica*. This little plant is notable on account of its round, shiny leaves, because the flowers are insignificant. It is a

The umbrella plant, Darmera peltata, *on the bank of a large pond, with a red-flowering* Astilbe.

nice plant to use for linking up groups of rather taller ground-cover plants, or to form a background for them. The umbrella plant, *Darmera peltata* (syn. *Peltiphyllum peltatum*), grows in sun as well as light shade. The pretty, pink flowers in April and May are followed by beautiful, shiny, round leaves that look very good along the edge of a pond.

The lovely, pale green foliage of the marsh fern, Thelypteris palustris.

Half shade   *Ajuga, Darmera, Gunnera, Lysimachia, Petasites, Thelypteris palustris.*
For damp areas that are not permanently wet can be added: *Adianthum pedatum, Asarum, Astilbe* (various species and cultivars), *Brunnera, Campanula portenschlagiana* and *P. poscharskyana, Ceratostigma, Dicentra, Epimedium, Hosta, Galium, Onoclea, Pulmonaria* and *Tiarella.*

Shrubs for slopes and large beds

In the previous chapters the emphasis has been mainly on perennials. They are the most suitable ground-cover plants for smaller gardens. A shrub often takes up a lot of room and a group of shrubs can quickly outgrow the available space.

Large beds   Many shrubs are regularly used as ground cover in parks and other public places. They fill in areas between the road, the cycle way, and footpath. They are often dull, and they must be tough to reduce the amount of maintenance. A few local authorities employ specialist landscape gardeners who include beds with bright roses or other flowering shrubs in their planting schemes. In parks it is very often utility that rules the day. Shrubs like this, such as the *Cotoneaster*, *Berberis*, and *Stephanandra* should be planted in a private garden in large groups only if the garden lends itself to this and they are being used in low-maintenance areas.

It would be nicer to plant ivy as ground cover. Make a choice of cultivars from the climbing *Hedera helix*, *H. hibernica*, and *H. colchica*. The former also has a taller shrub form, 'Arborescens.' Although the various cultivars of *Euonymus fortunei* are widely used in municipal parks and gardens, this shrub is appropriate for the private garden. You can combine it with other ground cover, preferably among taller shrubs and trees. The flowering quince, *Chaenomeles*, achieves quite a spread and is suitable only for beds of several square metres (yards). This early-flowering, attractive shrub can sometimes be placed on its own or as part of a small group. After flowering, however, it does look rather dull and only the scented fruits give it some

Mahonia x wagneri *'Fireflame' has lovely bronze leaves.*

interest in the autumn. It is of course well known as a wall shrub. The flowering quince can form an impenetrable thicket with its thorny stems, one reason why it is often used in public parks. The same applies to *Mahonia* — the foliage of some species and cultivars is a lovely bronze colour, especially when the shrub is regularly pruned.

Stephanandra incisa 'Crispa' is, apart from when in flower, rather dull and so less suitable for the private garden.

More colour More colour is desirable in a private garden than in a public open space. You can choose from a number of ground-cover roses. In general the botanical species flower only once in a season, after which they have attractive rosehips. Many of these roses have long branches and are therefore less suitable for the garden. Climbing roses, too, can be used for ground cover only if there is plenty of space. Some cultivars of roses are more compact and after the main flowering season will regularly produce more flowers. It is advisable to remove the dead flowers to stimulate further flowering. In this way no seed is set and their energy is channelled into new growth and further blooms.

The various species of *Spiraea* are suitable for less abundant colour. The shades are often rather muted and fit in best with plants that have a rather dry character — with grey foliage for instance.

TIP
You can get ideas for shrubs and perennials at the annual Chelsea Flower Show in London, each May, or by visiting a botanic garden. In the Netherlands the trade fair 'Plantarium' is held each autumn in Boskoop.

Slopes In general we come across slopes beside houses that have been built above the level of the surrounding land. The difference in height can be taken up with low stone walls, by sleepers, or wooden panels, but this is all quite expensive. For that reason the slope is usually left as it is.

Because the house stands above the general level of the ground, the water table will be far below the ground which will therefore be on the dry side. The soil around the house often consists of poor sand. It is important in that case to work at improving the soil. You can adapt the planting to the quality of the ground. Look through the previous chapters on the various types of soil to find suitable shrubs, climbing plants, and perennials.

Planting slopes A slope is often too steep for grass, that has to be mown regularly. So shrubs are often used for ground cover. Usually just one species is chosen and it gives the effect of a heavy frame surrounding a painting. It can be nice to break up the frame here and there with something else. That could be other shrubs, or a clump of climbing plants that trail down the slope, but perennials could be useful, too. Do not make the planting too fragmented or the groups of plants too small, because that

Apart from being a lovely climbing plant, the climbing hydrangea, Hydrangea petiolaris, *can be used as ground cover.*

TIP

When you buy roses always ask whether they will flower once, or go on flowering throughout the summer.

64

will look untidy. Besides, you must give thought to the maintenance of a sloping area, and too many different plants will only increase the work.

Shrubs and climbing plants for large beds and slopes

Chaenomeles (some species), *Cotoneaster* (some species), *Euonymus fortunei* (various cultivars), *Hedera* (various species and cultivars), *Hydrangea*, *Hypericum*, *Lonicera* (some species and cultivars), *Mahonia* (some species and cultivars), *Rosa* (some species and cultivars), *Rubus* (some species), *Salix*, *Spiraea* (some species), *Wisteria*.

Conifers for large beds and slopes

Juniperus (various species and cultivars), *Microbiota*, *Taxus*.

Juniper *and* Mahonia *together give a strong contrast.*
Following page:
A lovely combination of flowering bugle, ajuga *and young ivy leaves.*

Rosa *'New Dawn' is suitable as ground cover only in large beds or on slopes.*

65

The A to Z of plants for ground cover

In this chapter all the perennials, ferns, annuals, bulbs, tubers, and rhizomatous plants, shrubs, climbing plants, roses, and conifers are listed in alphabetical order.

Perennials that are suitable for ground cover

Acaena (pirri-pirri-bur)

This very low-growing, ground-cover plant, which spreads strongly, can be grown in full sun to light shade and in soil types from normal garden to poor sandy ones. The flowers are insignificant but the spiny seeds, in a pretty bunch, give the plant its ornamental value. The fine-toothed leaf adds to this.

The plant is suitable for large beds and also for small gardens, where it can serve as a replacement for grass with other low plants.

Acaena buchanii has blue-green leaves and yellow-green, spiny fruits. *A. magellanica* forms grey-green clumps.

A. microphylla is rather coarser and has greenish-brown burrs. The cultivar 'Copper Carpet', with reddish-brown foliage and red fruits, is particularly attractive. *A. novae-zelandiae* has reddish-purple fruits and green leaves with a bluish sheen. *A. anserifolia* has green leaves and strong runners. These plants are rather coarser than the previous species. They are also suitable for light shade.

Achillea (yarrow)

Most yarrows are medium to tall plants, with flat flowering heads, which are suitable for the border and make good cut flowers. *Achillea chrysocoma* has beautiful silver-grey foliage and golden-yellow flower heads, 15cm (6in) across, in June to

August. It likes sun and dry, not too poor soil.

Aegopodium (ground elder)

Ground elder is the most terrible weed that, once in the garden, causes havoc and has been the despair of many a gardener. It is highly invasive and if only a small piece of root is left after weeding a new plant will grow with long, white, creeping roots. Although it makes attractive ground cover with its white flower heads, it is not to be recommended. There is also a variegated cultivar, *Aegopodium podagraria* 'Variegata', which is sold by some nurseries, and is less invasive, otherwise it would have been taken off the market long ago. This fast-growing

*The foliage of the lady's mantle is
particularly attractive.*
Above: The variegated self-heal, Ajuga
reptans *'Burgundy Glow.'*
Right: Lady's mantle, Alchemilla mollis,
and ostrich fern.
Opposite page: Acaena affinis.

ground cover, with bright green leaves with white markings on the leaves, reaches 30cm (12in) and produces white flowering heads from June to August. This variegated ground elder will grow in both sun and shade and is not fussy about the kind of soil.

Ajuga (bugle)

This low ground-cover plant spreads by means of long runners. The foliage remains green until far into the winter. The upright flowering stems appear in May and June, crowned with wreaths of lip-flowers. Bugle can make a carpet to replace grass. It demands shade to half shade, and normal, not too dry, soil. *Ajuga pyramidalis* has bright blue

flowers, *A. reptans* bluish-purple. The cultivar 'Atropurpurea' has deep bronze-purple leaves, 'Delightful' white variegated leaves, the 'Multicolour' and 'Burgundy Glow' spotted leaves in various shades, all with blue flowers. For pink flowers choose 'Rosea', 'Pink Elf', and 'Purple Torch.' 'Alba' is a white-flowered cultivar.

Alchemilla (lady's mantle)

This beautiful ground-cover plant with yellow-green, delicate flowering heads likes sun to light shade and normal garden soil from wet to dry.
The best known is *Alchemilla mollis*, about 25cm (10in) high, reaching 50cm (20in) in flower. It has lovely round leaves which

are covered in soft hairs so that in the early morning or after a shower drops of water glisten on the leaves. A second burst of flowering can be achieved by cutting off the spent flowering heads.
A. vulgaris is smaller in all respects. *A. alpina* and *A. erythropoda* scarcely reach 15cm (6in) even in flower and the leaves of both are noticeably smaller than those of *A. mollis*. The leaf of *A. alpina* has a pretty silver edge. They make good ground cover for a rock garden or small garden.

Anaphalis (pearl everlasting)

The pearl everlasting, with its grey leaves and white or pale yellow, closely-packed flowers, makes very good ground cover.

Ajuga occurs *frequently in the wild.*

Above: The flowers of Anaphalis triplinervis, *pearl everlasting, can be dried for arrangements.*
Left: The beautiful white flowers of Anemone aconitifolium.

It flowers in May and June and likes sun and normal, preferably calcareous, garden soil, which can be on the dry side. It dries very well for flower arrangements. In full flower it reaches about 40cm (16in). *Anaphalis triplinervis* has white flowers and grey, woolly leaves. *A. margaritacea* is stouter and less grey and can also be grown in light shade. They cover the ground by means of root runners.

Anemone (anemone)

Apart from the tuberous anemone, which will be discussed later, there is a lovely white-flowered anemone which can be used as ground cover. This is *Anemone sylvestris*, about 30 cm (12in) high, that flowers in May and June. The cultivar 'Macrantha' has larger blooms than the species. Although *A. aconitifolium* (*Ranunculus aconitifolius*) reaches 60cm (24in), it is suitable for ground cover but only in a large bed. It resembles *A. sylvestris* with its white flowers. It likes a position in half shade and prefers damp, humus-rich ground.

Antennaria (cat's ears)

The cat's ear is suitable for large beds because it spreads strongly, but because it is not completely frost-hardy it is more suitable for rock gardens, for growing against walls, and particularly as ground cover between stepping stones. This tiny plant, which only reaches 15cm (6in)

including flower spike, has pretty narrow leaves that are green and hairy above and covered in grey hairs beneath. It has clumps of small flowers in May and June.

Antennaria likes a warm, sunny situation and light, well-drained soil. *A. dioica* itself is not always easy to obtain but the pink cultivars 'Nyewoods Variety' and 'Rosea' are. The former has very deep pink flowers. *A. dioica 'Alba'* is white.

Arabis (rock cress)

These free-flowering little plants that form mats, are very suitable for a sunny situation in normal, well-drained garden soil. They are used at the front of the border but also in the rock garden, on low walls, and on

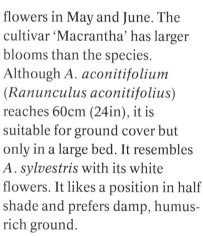

The foliage of Asarum caudatum, *wild ginger, is a lovely shiny green.*

Arabis procurrens, *rock cress, has lacy white flower heads.*

slopes. The plant is particularly attractive because it flowers quite early, in April and May, sometimes through to June. If *Arabis* becomes too straggly it can be trimmed back. It will soon grow again.

A. blepharophylla reaches about 20cm (8in), and has pretty dark-green leaves with hairy, grey edges. The most commonly grown is *A. caucasica*. It makes good ground cover with grey-green foliage above which the double or single flowers appear. Most cultivars have white flowers, 'Plena' has double white flowers, and 'Rosabella' pink.

A. procurrens forms a thick flat mat about 15 cm (6in) high. This, too, has white flowers, and there is also a variegated cultivar 'Variegata.'

Armeria (sea pink)

Sea pink, a grass-like perennial which has cushions of pink flowers on long stalks in May and June, looks pretty as an edging or on sandy slopes. It is not demanding, provided the soil is sandy and well-drained, and it is even at home in the dunes.

Every two or three years split up the plants and replant only the outer parts because the centre of the clump often dies off. *Armeria maritima* has pale pink flowers, but there are deep pink, red, lilac, purple, and white cultivars.

The grassy cushions grow to about 10cm (4in) in height, with the flower stems a further 10cm (4in). *A. pseudarmeria* is a larger plant, reaching a good 30cm (12in) in flower. It has pink flowers.

Asarum (wild ginger)

This plant deserves a place because of its foliage, as the flowers hide under the leaves. The creeping rootstock ensures an even 10cm (4in) high carpet in shade or half shade. It likes soil with plenty of humus. *Asarum europaeum* (asarabacca) is the most commonly used species, with dark, kidney-shaped, shining leaves, that die off in only the spring. *A. caudatum* is rather taller, 15cm (6in) at the most, and has lighter green leaves.

Astilbe (spirea)

These plants are often called spirea although the name

The leaf of Bergenia *'Sunningdale' becomes reddish-brown during the winter.*

Above: The very early-flowering edging plant, Aubrieta.

Left: The delicate foliage of Astilbe chinensis *'Pumila' makes a nice, thick carpet.*

Previous page: Thrift, Armeria maritima, *has lovely rounded flower heads.*

Opposite page: The pink-flowering elephant's ears, Bergenia.

actually belongs to a shrub. This is rather confusing, so as with all plants it is better to use the Latin name. Astilbes have plumes of flowers which, depending on the species, can be stiff or very loose in character. The most suitable species for ground cover is the lilac *Astilbe chinensis* 'Pumila.' It reaches about 20cm (8in) and needs sun or light shade, in a damp soil, preferably with plenty of humus. Yet the various hybrids of *A. simplicifolia* are good for ground cover, such as the pale pink 'Inshriach Pink' and the pink 'Sprite.' These reach 40cm (16in) and are in flower around July. At the same time the various *A. japonica* hybrids, at 50 to 70cm (20 to 28in) are suitable for large groups and thus more or less for ground cover.

Aubrieta

In the spring everyone is eager for colour in the garden. The *Aubrieta* hybrids are therefore very much appreciated in April and May, sometimes earlier, with their clusters of small flowers in shades ranging from pale pink to deep blue. The foliage is grey-green but there are variegated cultivars. These can look messy because the leaves are very small. The plant forms cushions about 10cm (4in) high. It likes sun and well-drained, sandy soil.

Bergenia (elephant's ears)

Elephant's ears prefers a position in sun or light shade, but the more sun the more prolific the pink, red, or white flowers.

The soil must be damp, but not wet, but the plant can stand periods of drought. Then you need to cover the exposed creeping rootstock with earth. The flowering season is March to April. The leaves are large and decorative and remain attractive in winter, especially if, as in some cultivars, they turn dark red. Elephant's ears can reach 40cm (16in).

Bergenia crassifolia has reddish leaves, *B. purpurascens* dark purple ones, but the hybrid,

'Sunningdale' is a magnificent reddish-brown in winter.

Brunnera (great forget-me-not)

The plant is attractive because of its bright blue flowers, which resemble the forget-me-not. The large, heart-shaped leaves make a nice contrast among delicate or dark-coloured foliage. There is also a variegated cultivar, *Brunnera macrophylla* 'Variegata', but this is not so strong and needs more light. *Brunnera* reaches 30 to 40cm (12 to 16in), and grows in ordinary, not too dry soil with plenty of humus, in half shade.

Campanula (bellflower)

There are over 200 different species. Not all are suitable for the climate in western Europe, but there are plants that are found in many gardens, among them several good ground-cover varieties. Most bellflowers like well-drained, fertile soil, but the low-growing ones will tolerate dry and therefore poor soil, in a sunny or half-shaded position. *Campanula carpatica* reaches about 20cm (8in) including flowers. The basin-shaped flowers appear in June and July, with often a second burst in late summer. This plant forms thick clumps, which, provided they are planted not more than 20—25cm (8—10in) apart, will cover the ground. *C. carpatica* has blue flowers, as does 'Blue Clips', but there are also white cultivars, for example 'Alba', and 'White Clips.' *C. cochleariifolia* is a lovely little plant for small gardens, where it spreads underground and flowers in June and July. It can cover the ground between stepping stones. In the rock garden, too, and on low walls and in hanging baskets this 10cm (4in) high plant is a real bonus, with its small, violet-blue, hanging flowers.

Another nice species is *C. portenschlagiana*, 10cm (4in) high, with small, funnel-shaped, violet flowers. It flowers in June and July with a second burst in late summer. It makes surface as well as underground runners and so forms a lovely carpet or hangs in a decorative curtain over the edge of a low wall.

C. poscharskyana is more suitable for larger beds, at least

The mouse ear, Cerastium, *has very bright, white flowers.*
Above: Campanulas *always make rewarding garden plants.*
Left: The little blue flowers of Ceratostigma.
Previous page: Astilbes *in various colours along the bank.*

1.5m (5ft) square, because it spreads very vigorously and has long, trailing stems. It reaches about 15cm (6in) and has star-shaped, deep blue flowers in June and July. After that the new shoots flower regularly. There are some good cultivars, including the lavender-pink 'Lisduggan Variety', the white 'E. H. Frost', and the mauve 'Stella.' The climbing, violet-blue 'Blauranke' is the most suitable for trailing over walls or for the edge of the bed to break up a large expanse of sleepers. *C. glomerata,* the clustered bellflower, is a good garden plant, not exactly a ground-cover plant but it can be used as such because a relatively closed cover of leaves develops after several years' growth. During the flowering season its bright blue can be rather obtrusive, at least if you choose the cultivar 'Superba', but the white-flowered 'Alba' will avoid this problem. The clustered bellflower grows to a height of 40cm (16in) and flowers from May to July. It prefers alkaline soil in sun or half shade. It is better to use *C. garganica* as ground cover — this only reaches 15cm (6in) — and has pale blue flowers from June to August.

Cerastium (mouse ear)

These strong, grey-leafed plants — suitable for full sun and a well-drained, fairly poor sandy soil — flower in June. There are several species of which *Cerastium biebersteinii* is the fastest grower and reaches 20cm (8in). This species must not be planted in small beds because it can soon choke its neighbours. It does, however, make good ground cover for slopes in the sun. *C. tomentosum* has smaller leaves, is rather lower, and less invasive. The most suitable for small beds is the even smaller *C. tomentosum* var. *columnea.*

Ceratostigma

Is this a shrub or a perennial? It is actually a shrub, because the plant is woody, but in western Europe it often dies off above ground in the winter and it is therefore included under the perennials. It is also put under sub-shrubs. It needs a sheltered, preferably warm, position in the

The yellow Corydalis lutea *also occurs in the wild.*

Above: The white bells of the lily-of-the-valley, Convallaria majalis, *hide among the leaves.*

Right: Cornus canadensis *makes good cover for moist ground.*

sun, and well-drained, sandy soil. It is a lovely plant, about 25cm (10in) high, with dark-green leaves that are grey-green beneath, so that the gentian-blue flowers that appear in August to October stand out beautifully. The foliage turns rich red in the autumn. The plant must have the space for the underground runners to extend. The most usual species is *Ceratostigma plumbaginoides*.

Chamaemelum (chamomile)

This relative of the Roman chamomile has a low, creeping growth habit. The finely divided leaves give off a strong, pleasant, scent when crushed between the fingers or under the feet. It is better not to walk on it too much because the plant can suffer

damage. *Chamaemelum nobile* 'Treneague' does not flower and is attractive on account of its lovely, deep-green, scented leaves which form a low, dense carpet. It is suitable for sun and half shade in fertile sandy soil.

Convallaria (lily-of-the-valley)

Everyone knows the lily-of-the-valley with its sweet scent that has romantic associations because it used to be very popular in wedding bouquets. With its underground runners lily-of-the-valley makes good ground cover in shade and half shade. The ground needs to be damp and to contain plenty of humus. The tiny, bell-shaped flowers are often rather dwarfed by the foliage.

Convallaria majalis flowers in

May. There is also a pink cultivar, a double variety 'Flore Pleno', and 'Variegata.' The ordinary white one is, however, the most vigorous.

Cornus (creeping dogwood)

Cornus canadensis is the only species that is grown as a perennial — the others are all woody shrubs, including the early spring-flowering dogwood, Cornelian cherry.

The one described here is a 20cm (8in) high plant that has pretty white flowers in June and July, sometimes followed by red fruits. The rather large leaves stand in whorls of four or six. This woodland plant, which in its native country grows under pine trees, likes peaty soil and prefers a position in light shade.

Dianthus deltoides, *the maiden pink, has several lovely cultivars, including this 'Flashing Light.'*
Above: The pink sprays of the umbrella plant are followed by large round leaves.
Left: Cotula squalida *can be used in place of grass.*

Corydalis

This is a very attractive plant, if only because of its delicate, fern-like leaves. The yellow-flowered *Corydalis lutea* grows in the wild — it reaches about 30cm (12in). It grows on walls and rocks in the shade, which shows that it prefers a situation in lime-rich soil in light shade, although it will grow in sun or shade and it is actually not too fussy about the soil.

C. ochroleuca, like *C. lutea*, flowers from May to October, with tufts of creamy-white flowers. It is a slightly taller plant, about 40cm (16in).

Cotula

With its leaf like a feathery moss, and a height of no more than 3cm (1 ¹/₂in), *Cotula* can replace grass. The turf can be walked on although not too frequently, and ball games are out of the question. The flower is unremarkable. *Cotula* will grow in any soil, provided it is not too dry, and in sun or half shade. *C. squalida* is the most popular, with its bronze foliage which can form a good contrast with green shades.

Darmera (umbrella plant)

The umbrella plant forms mats of thick roots which make it impossible for other plants to get established. Only a short length of root with an eye will provide a new plant. In April and May *Darmera peltata* (syn. *Peltiphyllum peltatum*) produces bunches of little pink flowers on long stalks. After the flowers come the large, shiny, round leaves on stalks 80—100cm (32—39in) long. The plant likes damp soil in half shade.

Dianthus (pink)

Many of the pinks are suitable for filling beds at the front of the border, but they can also be used as edging plants, as ground cover between roses, and in the rock garden. Pinks like a sunny position.

The maiden pink, *Dianthus deltoides*, has delicate, needle-like leaves, and flowers throughout the summer with pretty little flowers on stems about 15cm (6in) high. There is a white cultivar 'Albus', and the red 'Fanal' with a dark leaf. *D. deltoides* 'Flashing Light'

The leopard's bane, Doronicum, *flowers
with the bluebell.*

Dutchman's breeches, Dicentra, *is an
attractive perennial suitable for ground
cover.*

is a less well-known, bright
cerise, cultivar which is well
worth growing. The maiden
pink, in contrast to other pinks,
prefers acid soil. The *D.
plumarius* hybrids make good
ground cover with their grey-
green leaves. These prefer lime-
rich soil and that may be why
they are uncommon in some
areas. Yet they are attractive,
especially in combination with
other grey-leafed plants.
There are many hybrids,
together with single and double
forms in shades from white to
deep red.

Dicentra (Dutchman's breeches)

Is *Dicentra* a ground-cover
plant or not? The lower-growing
varieties can be included under
that heading. They form a pretty,
close carpet if they are planted
close enough together.
Dutchman's breeches is happiest
in cool, humus-rich sandy soil.
D. formosa is very suitable for
filling in beds in half shade. The
fern-like foliage is very pretty,
even apart from the little heart-
shaped flowers on slender,
arching stems. The number of
cultivars available is very wide,
including the carmine pink,
long-flowering 'Adrian Bloom',
the pink 'Bountiful', together
with the long-flowering dark red
'Luxuriant', and the white 'Pearl
Drops', with its blue-green
leaves.

Doronicum (leopard's bane)

Unfortunately the leaves of this
cheerful, yellow-flowered plant
become less attractive during the
summer. In April and May there
are bright yellow flowers on long
stalks above the bright green,
heart-shaped leaves. On dry soil
these can die off completely as
the summer progresses.
Doronicum is an excellent plant
for growing under shrubs and
trees because it can stand a lot of
shade. It stands out in spring,
and during the summer it is the
shrubs that attract attention.
In general the leopard's bane is
not fussy about the soil,
provided it is not too poor.
It will grow in sun or shade.
Doronicum spreads by means of
a creeping rootstock.
D. pardalianches has
naturalized in woods on old
country estates. This species can
have flowers on stalks up to

This relative of the strawberry, Duchesnea indica, *has flowers and fruit at the same time.*

Dryas *makes a very low ground-cover layer, with anemone-like flowers followed by plumes of seeds.*

70cm (28in) high. The lower-growing *D. orientale* is the most usual one grown. This reaches about 40cm (16in). The cultivar 'Spring Beauty' flowers freely with double, bright yellow heads. One of the loveliest is *D. plantagineum* 'Excelsum.'

Dryas (mountain avens)
This delightful, very low, mat-forming plant is suitable for small beds and rock gardens. Mountain avens prefers humus-rich, alkaline soil, and prefers a place in the sun. The 20cm (8in) high *Dryas octopetala* has lovely, cup-shaped, creamy-white flowers with a deep yellow centre from May to July. After flowering, the silver, silky seed heads develop, which in dry, sunny weather form a nice contrast against the dark green foliage. *D. x suendermannii* is even lower and flowers a month later. This is the hybrid that is mostly offered for sale, because the flower and leaf are larger and so the plant is more striking. The stems of this ground-cover plant become woody and for that reason it is also included under shrubs.

Duchesnea
This is a relative of the cultivated strawberry, but the small fruits of *Duchesnea indica* are tasteless. The flowers are yellow. The leaf is smaller than that of the strawberry, but both produce runners which develop new plants where they touch the ground at a leaf node. The plant can be invasive and so needs to be carefully watched, certainly in a moderate sized garden. It is not demanding as to soil conditions, provided they are not too heavy or wet, and will grow in sun, half shade or shade. It can also be used in hanging baskets.

Epimedium (barrenwort)
This makes excellent ground cover because of its creeping rootstock, and the foliage is attractive although the flowers are often hidden under the leaves. Because the foliage has often just died off it is advisable to trim the dead leaves to reveal the flowers, which grow on delicate stems. *Epimedium* likes a situation in shade or half shade, and humus-rich soil that does not become too dry.

The storksbill, Erodium variabile, *is suitable for small beds and rock gardens.*

Above: Beautifully marked leaf of Epimedium.
Right: The Epimedium *has very delicate flowers.*

There are various nice species and cultivars, such as the yellow-flowered *E. x perralchicum* 'Frohnleiten' with quite large flowers. *E. x rubrum*, as you would expect, has red flowers and particularly in spring is very attractive on account of its bright green leaves with bronze markings.
In the autumn the foliage turns red. *E. versicolor* 'Sulphureum' has lovely, sulphur-yellow flowers. Good white forms are *E. grandiflorum* and *E. youngianum* 'Niveum.' Both have pink cultivars — 'Rose Queen' and 'Roseum' respectively. There are also orange and copper-coloured types available, including *E. x warleyense* and *E. pinnatum* ssp. *colchicum*.

Epimedium varies in height between 20—30cm (8—12 in).

Erodium (Storksbill)

These plants which resemble *Geranium* are very suitable for the rock garden and drier places. They flower from May onwards. Their lovely leaves need protection during severe frost. They like a sunny position. Good species and cultivars include the white with a black centre *Erodium guttatum*, the deep pink *E. variabile* 'Bishop's Form', the two pink cultivars 'County Park', and 'Roseum.' Most of them do not exceed 10 to 20cm (4 to 8in).

Euphorbia (spurge)

There are many species of spurge, but only a few are

suitable for ground cover. All spurges have a white sap which is exuded when the plant is damaged.
Wood spurge, *Euphorbia amygdaloides*, is useful. It is a roughly 60cm (24in) evergreen, native plant which has yellowish-green flowers form April to June. The cultivar 'Purpurea' has brownish foliage. Although most spurges prefer full sun, the wood spurge, together with the variety *robbiae*, can stand quite a lot of shade.
E. cyparissius has creeping rootstocks out of which grow the 25cm (10in) or so high stems with the very fine leaves.
On poor soil in full sun this sometimes turns a lovely orange colour. It flowers in April and

In the wild Euphorbia cyparissias *and the bladder campion grow together on poor ground.*

Right: The leaf of Fragaria *'Baron von Solenmacher' makes a nice, bright green carpet.*

Opposite page: Euphorbia amygdaloides *also occurs in the wild.*

May. *E. myrsinites* has long, prostrate stems with thick, fleshy leaves. It is actually a rock plant, but can also be used as ground cover in moderate sized beds. It only reaches 20cm (8in) in height and in May and June has the yellow-green flowers on the end of the stems. The "flowers" are actually the flowers proper plus the surrounding red bracts. The plant needs full sun and well-drained soil.

Fragaria (strawberry)

The cultivated strawberry can, of course, be used as ground cover but the quality of the fruit is likely to be lower because the fruit lacks sun owing to the dense foliage and the fruit can be affected by pests. Harvesting will be more difficult, too. The wild strawberry, *Fragaria vesca*, has white flowers and edible fruit, albeit small ones. The cultivar 'Alexandria' has larger fruit. 'Alba' is a white-fruited cultivar. The wild strawberry likes fertile soil in sun or half shade. There is a new cross between *Fragaria* and a *Potentilla* — the *Fragaria* 'Pink Panda' — a lovely plant with sugar-pink flowers which, however, will spread less vigorously than the strawberry. This newcomer likes full sun and normal, well-drained soil.

Galium (woodruff)

Galium odoratum, formerly *Asperula odorata*, has whorled, lance-shaped leaves, which are a beautiful, lush green in spring. In April it bears bunches of delicate, white flowers, likes half shade, and damp, humus-rich soil, which may also contain lime. Bunches are used in making May Bowl and dried stems are used among clothes, not only because of the scent but to discourage moths.

Geranium (cranesbill)

The choice of cranesbills is enormous, and there is a range between attractive foliage and pretty flowers. There are low, almost creeping cranesbills, tall species that make good plants for the border, and species that are very suitable as ground cover for large areas. Generally speaking, cranesbills can be grown in any normal garden soil in sun to half shade, and a few species tolerate more shade. *Geranium cantabrigiense*

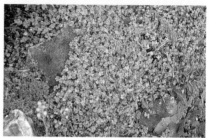

The tiny leaf of Geranium dalmaticum *turns colour beautifullly.*
Above: Geranium macrorrhizum 'Ingwersen's Variety.'
Left: The bloody cranesbill, Geranium sanguineum, *also has a white cultivar,* 'Alba.

'Biokovo' grows no more than 15cm (6in) high, with lovely, small, light-green leaves. It flowers in May and June and the white flowers have pink stamens. Even on dry ground this cranesbill will form a lovely carpet.

G. cinereum also remains low, 10—15cm (4—6in), and flowers in July and August. The cultivar 'Ballerina' is lovely, with purplish-pink flowers that have darker veins.

G. cinereum var. *subcaulescens* has bright purple-magenta flowers, the cultivar 'Splendens' striking carmine pink ones. Another lovely low-growing species is *G. dalmaticum*, which scarcely reaches 10cm (4in) and is very suitable for planting between stones and in the rock garden, even on poor, rather dry ground. In June and July it has pale shell-pink flowers which darken with age. The anthers are red.

G. macrorrhizum is noticeably taller, 25—40cm (10—16in). The pretty, light-green leaf is round and coarsely toothed. The plant bears rather small flowers in June and July. There are various lovely cultivars such as 'Album', white with pink stamens, 'Velebit', which is deep pink, and 'Spessart', very pale pink to almost white, with pink stamens. 'Ingwersen's Variety', a soft rose-pink, has aromatic leaves that turn colour in the autumn.

G. nodosum is a lovely species because it can also grow in dry places in the shade, where its foliage makes a splash of bright green. The lilac-pink flowers are not very numerous but they do last a long time. The plant goes on producing flowers after the main season in June and July.

G. sanguineum, bloody cranesbill, can also tolerate drought, but needs sun, so that with its prostrate stems it can make a lovely, 25cm (10in) thick carpet and grow prettily over the edge of low walls. The leaf is slightly shiny and dark-green with a diameter of 5—10cm (2—4in). The flowers, which come out in June and July, are carmine pink. There are several valuable cultivars including the white 'Album' (20cm) (8in), the dark carmine pink 'Max Frei' (15cm) (6in), and the bright pink variety *striatum* (10cm) (4in).

The variegated cultivar of the ground ivy
is very suitable for growing with annuals.
Above: Glechoma hederacea, *ground ivy,*
is a pretty blue herb.
Right: Geranium endressii *and its cultivar*
'Wargrave Pink' have a rather untidy
growth.

G. wallichianum 'Buxton's Variety' also has prostrate stems which makes it suitable for ground cover.

Unfortunately it is not reliably winter hardy, but for anyone who wants blue flowers, it is worth trying. Put it in a somewhat sheltered place. There are many species of *Geranium* suitable for large beds, such as the pink *G. endressii*, its cultivar 'Wargrave Pink', and the beautiful blue-flowering *G. himalayense*, but they are not true ground-cover plants. *G. renardii* is worth the effort — it is particularly attractive on account of its lovely grey-green, hairy leaves, against which the white flowers with violet veining are shown off to advantage. This cranesbill grows to about 25cm (10in) and flowers in June and July.

Geum (avens)

The wild *Geum rivale*, water avens, has a few nice cultivars with hanging, bell-shaped flowers that appear in May and June. They grow no higher than about 40cm (16in). *Geum* grows best in the sun or half shade and in a rather damp, humus-rich soil. Pretty cultivars include the white 'Album', the pink 'Leonard', and the shrimp-red 'Lionel Cox.'

Glechoma (ground ivy)

This nice ground-cover plant is often regarded as a weed because of its ability to spread strongly. *Glechoma hederacea* makes long, above-ground runners that root easily and from this node further runners develop. The foliage, among which violet-blue flowers appear in April and May, is shiny and heart-shaped. The plant is most at home in light shade but can also thrive in full sun, but only if the ground is fairly damp. Any soil is suitable, provided it is not too dry. There is also *G. hederacea* 'Variegata.' This is commonly used as a house plant, and also in containers among annuals in the summer.

Gunnera

The best-known *Gunnera* is everything except ground cover, being a solitary plant with huge leaves that can reach a height of 2m (6ft). The less well-known *G. magellanica* is, in contrast,

The creeping Gypsophila *repens 'Rosea.'*
Right: The rock rose 'Wisley Pink.'

Previous page: The water avens, Geum
rivale, *has a lovely, deep-pink cultivar,*
'Leonard.'

only 15 cm (6in) high and has
lovely, round shiny leaves.
It likes a damp soil and light
shade. It is not completely
winter-hardy.

Gypsophila

The strongly divided stem and
the many, tiny flowers of
Gypsophila make a nice
contrast among perennials with
a coarser foliage and flowers.
The low-growing species are
suitable for the rock garden or
the front of a border.
Gypsophila likes sun and a dry,
preferably lime-rich, soil.
It flowers in June and July.
G. repens reaches about 20cm
(8in) and has white flowers. The
double 'Pink Star' is pink, as is
'Rosea' and the pale pink, rather
taller 'Veil of Roses'. The pink

'Pink Beauty' and the white
striped with rose *G. cerastioides*
are only 10cm (4in)tall and are
suitable for small gardens.

Helianthemum (rock rose)

Although the rock rose develops
woody stems and therefore
strictly comes under shrubs, it is
included under perennials here
because that is where it can
often be found in nurseries and
garden centres, if not under rock
plants. It is a very attractive,
evergreeen shrub for a sunny
spot. It is not really a ground-
cover plant but can be used as
such because the twigs are
prostrate. It likes well-drained
soil, which can be on the dry
side. Most cultivars grow to 15
to 20cm (6 to 8in) high and
flower in shades ranging from

white through yellow and
orange to deep red, single or
double.
They flower throughout the
summer. 'Amabile Plenum' is a
double red cultivar, 'Ben Hope'
carmine-red, the double 'Cerise
Queen' is rose pink, and
'Golden Queen' is golden-
yellow. The loveliest white
cultivar is 'Snow Queen.' 'Wisley
Pink' has grey-green leaves and
little pink flowers.

Hepatica (liverleaf)

This semi-evergreen plant for
shade or half shade reaches no
more than 15cm (6in) in height.
It is a rather delicate plant that
cannot cope with invasive
competitors, which soon cause it
to disappear. It is fussy about
soil, too.

Heuchera brizoides '*Schneewittchen.*'

Above: The hawkweed, Hieracium aurantiacum.

Left: The leaf of Heuchera micrantha '*Palace Purple*' *contrasts very well with the cream-coloured flowers.*

This must be humus-rich and contain lime.

The leathery leaf of *Hepatica transsylvanica* is five-lobed and often toothed. This is the most common species, with pretty blue flowers in March and April. Other species that can be found in specialized nurseries are *H. americana* and *H. nobilis*, mostly blue, but there are white and pink cultivars.

Herniaria (rupturewort)

This fast-growing, delicate, little plant can be used as a replacement for grass because it remains very small.

Herniaria glabra flowers from June to September, with clusters of tiny, yellow-green flowers. The plant needs good, well-drained soil, sun and light shade.

Heuchera and x Heucherella

Heucherella resulted from a cross between *Heuchera* and *Tiarella cordifolia*. *Tiarella* is a true ground-cover plant, but *Heuchera* is not, although this plant can, if planted closely enough, fill large beds. Both plants like half-shade and well-drained, fertile soil.

Heuchera x brizoides has pretty bell-shaped flowers on stems about 50cm (20in) long.

The roundish leaves form a close carpet. There are various lovely cultivars, such as the red 'Rain of Fire' and the white 'Schneewittchen.'

Heuchera micrantha 'Palace Purple' has become more common recently. It has larger, more indented reddish-brown leaves, and white flowers.

Heucherella has similar flowers to *Heuchera* and the creeping growth habit of the other parent, *Tiarella*. *Heucherella alba* 'Bridget Bloom' and the less well known *H. tiarelloides* produce pink flowers all through the summer.

Hieracium (hawkweed)

The hawkweed is really a wild plant but it makes an attractive garden plant because of its warm, orange colouring. It does best in a position in sun to light shade, and in dry, sandy soil. It spreads rapidly by root runners and also seeds freely, soon becoming naturalized.

Hieracium aurantiacum, orange hawkweed, is actually a garden escape, now naturalized. It forms very flat leaf rosettes,

The white flowers of Houttuynia cordata.

Above: The white-rimmed foliage of
Hosta undulata *'Albomarginata.'*
Right: The leaves of the hostas are very
variable. This is the gold and green of
Hosta fortunei *'Albopicta.'*

with the 20cm (8in) flower heads rising out of them. It has bright copper-orange flowers on 20cm (8in) stems from May to October. The mouse-ear hawkweed, *H. pilosella* has yellow flowers.

Hosta

There are many lovely species and cultivars to choose from for ground cover — green, grey-green, blue-green, and also many variegated ones. The hostas, which deserve a place in every garden on account of their decorative foliage, often also have attractive flowers — white or various shades of mauve. These are slender, funnel-shaped, and stand on long stalks. The majority flower in July and August, the odd species later or rather longer. The plant can grow in sun or shade or half shade. It will flower more abundantly in the sun. The soil must be fertile and fairly damp, especially if the plant is growing in full sun. The taller-growing hostas are also suitable for ground cover but only in very large gardens, where they can form imposing groups.

The smaller species can be used as ground cover in smaller gardens, with the taller ones as a specimen plant here and there. The leaves of hosta are almost indispensable for flower arranging. The following is a small selection from what is available.

Hosta clausa var. *normalis* has violet flowers and small green leaves and forms runners, a true ground cover plant. It grows to about 50cm (20in). *H. lancifolia* and *H. nakaiana* both have purple flowers. The former has narrow green leaves about 60cm (24in) long, the latter reaches no more than 30cm (12in).

The species with blue-grey leaves are particularly nice, such as *H. tardiana* 'Halcyon', 50cm (20in) high, and *H. fortunei* 'Hyacynthina', 60cm (24in) with purple flowers. There are many variegated hostas. Again, a small selection. Good examples of the *H. fortunei* cultivars are the golden-variegated 'Aureomarginata', the yellow-spotted 'Albopicta', the white-edged 'Moerheim' and 'Marginato-Alba.' They all reach about 70cm (28in). There are some good variegated cultivars

Hosta sieboldiana *'Elegans' has large blue-green leaves.*
Above: The very low ground-cover plant Hydrocotyle novae-*zelandiae likes damp ground.*
Left: Hylomecon japonicum *is pretty only for a short time.*

in other species such as *H. undulata* 'Albomarginata' with a white edge to the leaf, 'Mediovariegata' with green and white leaves, like 'Univittata.' The latter grows to only 40cm (16in), the rest to 60—70cm (24—28in).

Houttuynia

This is a good ground-cover plant, albeit with a tendency to become invasive. It spreads by means of a creeping rootstock. It is suitable for shade and half shade and needs damp, fertile ground.
Houttuynia cordata has pretty, heart-shaped leaves, above which the white flowers appear in May and June. There is also a double cultivar, 'Plena.' 'Chameleon' has a leaf which is

prettily marked in green, cream, and red.

Hydrocotyle (pennywort)

This very low ground-cover plant (5cm) (2in) likes moisture — hence "hydro" which means water. It also likes sun. The small, round, shiny leaves are particularly attractive. It has yellow-green flowers in August, but they are unremarkable. *Hydrocotyle novae-zeelandiae* is the usual species.

Hylomecon

This relative of the poppy is a nice plant for fertile soil in half shade. Unfortunately after the flowers are over the leaves often die off, but if you want something a bit different, it is nice among other ground cover,

under shrubs or trees. *Hylomecon japonicum* reaches 25cm (10in) and has golden-yellow flowers in April and May.

Lamium (deadnettle)

In the wild you come across the white deadnettle which is quite pretty but not very exciting once it has flowered. There are, however, several nice species and cultivars in cultivation which are suitable for ground cover for the more wild garden, where they can be planted under trees and shrubs, because they do very well in half shade and shade in any normal, not too dry soil.
Lamium maculatum reaches about 20cm (8in) and has dark-green leaves with a white to silver fleck. It has reddish-purple

Lamium galeobdolon *'Silver Carpet' has
a very delicately marked leaf and pretty
yellow flowers.*
*Above: The wild form of the yellow
archangel,* Lamium galeobdolon.
Right: Bird's foot trefoil, Lotus
corniculatus.

flowers from June to August.
There are various good cultivars,
such as the white 'Album', and
'White Nancy' with silver
variegated foliage, the pink
'Roseum', the soft 'Shell Pink',
and the red 'Chequers' and
'Silver Dollar.' 'Beacon Silver' is
very delicate, with very striking
silver leaves and little pink
flowers.
L. galeobdolon (syn.
Lamiastrum galeobdolon) is
only suitable for large areas
because it can run wild and
choke the neighbouring plants.
The long, creeping stems with
the variegated leaves root at the
nodes and form new plants. It is
suitable for any kind of soil,
prefers shade or half shade, has
yellow flowers in May and June,
and reaches about 25cm (10in).

There are a few nice cultivars
that are less invasive and that
have nicely marked leaves, for
example 'Hermann's Pride', or
'Silver Carpet.' These, too, have
yellow flowers.

Lithodora

Lithodora is a long-flowering
and sun-loving plant for a well-
drained, preferably calcareous
soil. The plant is not totally
winter-hardy and during hard
frosts it needs some protection.
Lithodora diffusa 'Alba' has
white flowers, and 'Cambridge
Blue' light blue flowers, but the
loveliest is the cultivar
'Heavenly Blue', with beautiful
clear blue flowers from May to
July.
The lance-shaped leaves are
dark green.

Lotus (bird's-foot trefoil)

This plant, which is also found
in the wild, makes a nice ground
cover with its long, prostrate
stems. It prefers sun, but can
tolerate some shade and likes
dry ground. The leaves are very
delicate. The flowering season is
from June to September.
The double form is *Lotus corni-
sculatus* 'Plenus.'

Lysimachia (creeping Jenny)

There are several species, but
although they often put out
runners they are not always
suitable for ground cover,
because their growth is not
compact enough or too tall.
Lysimachia nummularia,
sometimes known as
moneywort, makes long,
twining, growths which root

— it is good as ground cover. It grows in sun as well as shade and likes damp, humus rich soil. It reaches 10cm (4in) and has butter-yellow flowers from May to August.

Maianthemum (May lily)

May lily is a real connoisseur's plant. It is not very striking and needs some care because it is very delicate. The foliage dies off at the end of the summer. *Maianthemum bifolium* can tolerate a lot of shade and occurs in the wild, under shrubs and trees on a moist, but not too wet soil. It has heart-shaped leaves, ending in a long point, above which in May the bunches of white flowers stand out, occasionally followed by red berries.

Mazus

This slightly unusual plant is suitable for ground cover, among stepping stones, and in the rock garden, where it will creep over stones with its long stems and hang decoratively from low walls. It likes half shade and not too dry soil. Severe, wet winters are disastrous for this nice little plant. You need to provide some protection in the winter and give it a place where water does not stand even after heavy rain. *Mazus reptans*, blue-purple, is the species most often seen in nurseries but there is also a white cultivar, 'Albus.' The flowers resemble toadflax.

Melissa (Lemon balm)

Lemon balm has a creeping rootstock and rather

Melissa officinalis '*Aurea.*'

unremarkable flower heads. Like the mints it releases a strongly-scented essential oil when the leaves are bruised, in this instance lemon-scented. Lemon balm is well known as a culinary herb and another name, "bee herb" testifies to its importance for scented honey production.

The ordinary *Melissa officinalis* is not so suitable for the border because it does spread rapidly, and it is not particularly attractive later in the season. The cultivars 'Aurea' and 'Variegata', however, with their golden-yellow and golden-variegated leaves respectively, make a splash of colour, especially between green-leafed

Oenothera missouriensis *gives colour to the garden.*

Right: Omphalodes verna *has forget-me-not flowers very early in the year.*
Following page: A collection of various species of mint, Mentha.

plants. The variegated cultivars like sun or light shade and are not fussy about the soil, provided it is fairly damp.

Mentha (mint)

Anyone who has one of the many species of mint in the garden will know that they are almost all invasive, because of their spreading rootstocks. The lowest ones make good ground cover, but in general they do need space. Only *Mentha requienii*, Corsican mint, is less invasive and because of its low growth, 2cm (1\2in), can be used between stepping stones. It prefers a cool place, in light shade, with damp soil. All mints release essential oils when bruised. Corsican mint smells strongly of peppermint.

M. pulegium, pennyroyal, is a good 30cm (12in) high ground-cover plant, which needs protection from hard frosts. The lilac flowers are unremarkable.

Nepeta (catmint)

Although catmint is not a true ground-cover plant there are species that are suitable. Some species have very weak stems so that the plants are semi-prostrate and form a big clump. If they are planted 40 to 50 cm (16 to 20in) apart they will soon cover the surface. Catmint likes sun and normal to dry soil, which must not be water-logged in winter. The plant attracts bees. The scent given off by the leaves attracts cats, who love to roll in it.
Nepeta x faassenii is a grey-

leafed plant about 30cm (12in) high. The small, blue flowers open in loose spikes from June until late August, with some even into September. The cultivar 'Six Hills Giant' is more lilac-blue and reaches 50cm (20in), 'Snowflake' is white. This is only 30cm (12in) high. The 50cm (20in) 'Walkers Low' has dark-blue flowers. *N. mussinii* can be used as ground-cover. It is 30cm (12in) high with blue flowers.

Oenothera (evening primrose)

Most evening primrose species have too lax a form to make useful ground cover but *Oenothera macrocarpa* (syn. *O. missouriensis*) is an exception. It is only 15—20cm

(6—8in) high. Evening primroses like sun and well-drained soil which can even be somewhat sandy.

O. macrocarpa has large, yellow flowers from June to September. When planted in a large patch they make a very colourful impression when the flowers open at sundown.

Omphalodes

This pretty, early-flowering ground-cover plant likes shady, fertile, well-drained soil. It is a woodland plant with a creeping rootstock and so is very suitable for an under layer round trees and shrubs, where it will soon form a carpet.

Omphalodes verna reaches about 15cm (6in) and in April and May has tiny flowers like forget-me-nots. There is a white cultivar, 'Alba.' The plant is also attractive after flowering because of the heart-shaped leaves with a pale-green under surface.

Origanum (marjoram)

The various cultivars of this culinary herb are worth using as an ornamental plant in the garden. Like most herbs, marjoram likes a place in the sun and good, well-drained, soil with lime.

The compact *Origanum vulgare* 'Compactum' is very suitable for large beds, like the golden form 'Aureum' and the red-flowered 'Rosenkuppel.'

'Compactum' has tiny, lilac-pink flowers in clusters from June to August.

Oxalis (wood sorrel)

Oxalis acetosella is a very nice little plant that occurs in the wild in damp places in woods, but that can stand a fair amount of drought. It has pretty, pale-green, trifoliate leaves. In April and May the pale pink flowers appear above them, with the odd flower visible even into the summer. The flowers are not spectacular but quite attractive.

Pachysandra

This outstanding, evergreen ground-cover plant is at its best when planted in large beds. It likes humus-rich, well-drained soil and shade or half-shade. It has a fleshy rootstock out of which the shoots come, with a crown of oval leaves.

Pachysandra terminalis is the

The leaf of the butterbur, Petasites hybridus, *can reach the height of a man.*

Right: The sun makes patterns among the leaves of the butterbur, Petasites hybridus. *Opposite page: The wood sorrel has attractive little flowers.*

most common species. It grows to 20cm (8in) and has spikes of white flowers in April and May. There is also a cultivar 'Variegata.'

Petasites (butterbur)

The butterbur, *Petasites hybridus* is a very common sight along river banks and water features, where it forms large patches. It looks lovely in the wild, but you need to be careful in the garden situation because it is a ruthless invader that, particularly in the shade, can grow to an enormous height. Most species like a place in the sun or half shade on damp soil. There are also species that are less demanding of space but even they need quite a lot of space. *P. albus*, for example,

only reaches 25cm (10in), and unfurls its light-green leaves only after the white flowers have appeared in March and April. *P. fragrans*, too, is only 25cm (10in) high and has rose-pink flowers in late winter or early spring. This sweet-scented species is not, however, completely winter hardy.

Phlox

When you mention phlox, people immediately think of the tall border plants that flower in late summer, with their white to dark red or mauve flowers. Those are the *Phlox paniculata* hybrids. There is however, a ground covering species, *P. subulata*, whichgrows only to 10—15cm (4—6in), and flowers in April and May. These plants,

which form carpets, have delicate, needle-like leaves. They prefer sun and dry, sandy to fertile soil. In the flowering season the plant is covered with star-shaped flowers which almost cover the foliage. There is a large number of cultivars, such as the dark-purple 'Atropurpurea', the lilac-blue 'Bonita' and 'G. F. Wilson', the white 'May Snow', the pink 'Marjorie', and the scarlet 'Scarlet Flame.' But there are many others, all variations on white through pink to bright to deep red, and from pink to lilac to purple.

Phuopsis

Phuopsis is a relative of the woodruff, and they have a family resemblance. The leaves of

The plumes of Polygonum affine '*Donald Lowndes*' *are fatter than those of the species.*

Left: Polygonum bistorta, *bistort, is at home on the river bank.*

Opposite page: On fertile soil Phuopsis stylosa *flowers very freely*

Phuopsis are whorled and the flowers form a round head. *P. stylosa* (syn. *Crucianella stylosa*) has pink flowers in June to August and reaches about 30cm (12in). It forms mats on damp sandy soil in sun or light shade. It can also thrive in well-dug clay soil.

Polygonatum (Solomon's seal)

This plant, with its thick rootstock, is usually included under perennials, but it can also come under the rhizomatous plants. These are included in their turn with the bulbs and tubers which can be confusing. When Solomon's seal likes the conditions it will form a thick mat of roots above which the long, drooping stalks grow with their large, grey-green leaves. The white tubular flowers hang in groups of two to six. The plant flowers in May and June and prefers damp, humus-rich soil in half shade. The height of *Polygonatum multiflorum* depends very much on the soil, but it can reach 1m (3ft). *P. odoratum* is smaller. There is a cultivar of *P. multiflorum* available, 'Variegata.'

Polygonum (knotweed)

Species of *Polygonum* (syn. *Persicaria*) come in all shapes and sizes, from creeping to very long trailing ones. The low-growing ones make ground cover. They are not fussy about the soil, provided it is not too dry, and prefer sun or half shade. *P. affine* reaches about 20cm (8in), and flowers from June until the winter with long clusters of white flowers, which become pink as they age. The leaves are lance-shaped and survive until the worst frosts. There are a few nice cultivars, such as 'Darjeeling Red' which is rose-pink, the pink 'Donald Lowndes', and 'Superbum' which is pink becoming red. Occasionally you will come across *P. vaccinifolia*, a creeping, 25cm (10in) high plant with small, dark-green leaves and pink spikes from August to October. *P. bistorta*, common bistort, is taller, with quite large leaves and long stems with pretty, pink flower spikes. It prefers rather damp, humus-rich soil and a sunny to half shady position. It is lovely for

The pink-flowered self-heal, Prunella webbiana *'Rosea.'*

The flower heads resemble little beehives.

large areas, for instance along the water or on the edge of a wood.

Potentilla (cinquefoil)

The family consists of a large number of species that all make excellent plants for the border or the rock garden. A few of them have a growth form that makes them suitable for ground cover. There is also a group of shrubs among the potentillas. Most cinquefoils like a sunny position and well-drained soil that can be on the dry side.

Potentilla alba is 15cm (6in) high, with pretty grey-green leaves and white flowers in May and June. *P. sterilis* also has white flowers, but is taller, at 40cm (16in). Another low-growing species is *P. x tonquei*, with a pale orange which has a red centre. It is only 5cm (2in) high. *P. tridentata* (syn. *Sibbaldiopsis tridentata*) is only 10cm (4in) high and flowers in May and June with tiny, white, star-shaped flowers. It has pretty silver-grey foliage. Other cinquefoils can be used to fill large beds but are not true ground-cover plants.

Prunella (self-heal)

In the wild this lovely plant often occurs in grassland where it forms a dense mat. That is the species *Prunella vulgaris* which has blue flowers. Self-heal will grow on any well-drained soil, and it likes sun to half shade. The flowers look like tiny beehives. It grows to no more than 20cm (8in) and so it is ideal for filling large areas, for example beside paths and terraces. Some species and cultivars are: *P. grandiflora* with blue flowers, a white cultivar 'Alba', and the lilac-blue 'Loveliness.' *P. webbiana* 'Rosea' is pink.

Pulmonaria (lungwort)

Lungwort is a low-growing perennial that is very suitable for ground cover among shrubs because it does extremely well in shade and light shade. It likes good, humus-rich soil which must be damp but not wet. The attraction of this plant is that it flowers early. The first heads appear in March and they are all over by the end of May. The leaves, often spotted, more or less determine the height of the

Soapwort, Saponaria ocymoides.

Above: Raoulia australis *looks like a little silver cushion.*
Right: The rich flowers of the pearlwort, Sagina subulata.

plant. They are 20—30cm (8—12in), and lance-shaped. *Pulmonaria angustifolia* has green leaves and pretty blue flowers. *P. rubra* has pale green leaves and red flowers. *P. saccharata* has a cultivar 'Picta', "painted", a reference to the spotted leaves. Depending on the cultivar the marks vary from tiny specks to large patches. The best-known is 'Mrs Moon.' The flowers of the variegated lungwort are rose-pink fading to blue. During the flowering season the leaves and the varying flower colours make a splash of colour in the shade. *P. saccharata* has lilac-pink flowers, the cultivar 'Leopard' red ones. In *P. longifolia* (that is "having long leaves"), the leaves are also spotted but it is not always so obvious. In the white-flowered cultivar of *P. rubra*, 'Sissinghurst White', the spots are very clear.

Raoulia

Raoulia forms a mat of silver-grey leaves. It grows no higher than 5cm (2in). It prefers a sunny position and well-drained soil which does not become too wet in winter. The tiny, yellow flowers are not very noticeable. Look for *Raoulia australis* in nurseries specializing in rock plants.

Sagina (pearlwort)

This mossy little plant, only 5cm (2in) high, makes a good substitute for grass because it is itself bright green. It can be walked on but not too frequently or it will be damaged, although it does recover quite quickly. The stiff, pointed leaves which grow on stiff stalks are very tiny. The plant likes a sunny to half shade position on fertile soil, preferably sandy, but not too dry. The centre of the clump will rise up and lose contact with the soil so it is a good idea now and then to press it back. *Sagina subulata* is one of the few species grown here. It has tiny white flowers from June to August.

Saponaria (soapwort)

Both names are derived from the fact that the roots were used in the making of soap. *Saponaria ocymoides* is a 15cm (6in) high plant with many branched, prostrate stems, which in May

The skullcap, Scutellaria incana, *is also suitable for well-worked clay soil.*
Right: A detail of the flower of Saxifraga stolonifera *'Cuscutiformis.'*
Opposite page: London pride, Saxifraga x urbium, *as ground cover between the ostrich fern and* Centaurea montana.

and June are covered with a profusion of bright crimson flowers. This soapwort likes sun and well-drained, preferably lime-rich sandy soil or light garden soil. This species is useful as an edging plant, and as ground cover between rocks, and in the rock garden, creeping over stones and low walls.

Saxifraga (saxifrage)

There are a great many saxifrages to choose from. Most of them are most suitable for the rock garden but there some which can be used as ground cover in large beds. The *Saxifraga x arendsii* hybrids form 5cm (2in) high mats with very fine, mossy leaves. In April and May the flowers appear on taller, delicate stalks. They make the area into a carpet of flowers. This group likes sun, but will tolerate light shade, and needs well-drained, but slightly damp, soil. There are different cultivars with white, or pink through to red, flowers. They are suitable for rock gardens and smaller beds. London Pride, *S. x urbium*, is a pretty, evergreen ground-cover plant for shade and half shade in humus-rich, fairly damp soil. The thick leaves form rosettes and the plant quickly forms a good carpet, about 10cm (4in) high by means of runners. In May and June the slender flower stems develop with their delicate white flowers. The cultivar 'Clarence Elliot' is pink, like the 'Variegata.' The latter needs more light to bring out the variegation in the leaf.

Scutellaria (skullcap)

There are several members of this genus that are suitable for ground cover. This rock and border plant prefers well-drained soil in a sunny position. The most common garden species is *Scutellaria incana*, blue-flowered and 60cm (24in) high, so quite tall for ground cover. In some nurseries there is a wider selection, including the 5cm (2in) high *S. hastifolia* which has blue flowers. On some soils it can become invasive. *S. scordiifolia*, 15cm (6in) high, has violet-blue flowers.

Sedum (stonecrop)

There is a wide selection of stonecrops, but they do not all make good ground cover. They

The white-flowered stonecrop, Sedum album *'Murale.'*

A bed filled with various species of Sempervivum, *houseleek.*

like a sunny position and well-drained, garden soil, which can even be rather dry in summer. There are some good species for sandy soil, too. *Sedum acre*, biting stonecrop, forms lovely carpets of star-shaped, yellow flowers on very poor soils and in the dunes. *S. album* also forms a thick, very low carpet of tiny, round leaves above which the bunches of white flowers appear in May and June.

There are some pretty cultivars, such as 'Coral Carpet', with red leaves, and 'Murale' which has brown leaves and pink flowers. *S. kamtschaticum* grows to about 7cm (3in) and has red, prostrate stems that form a nice carpet, provided the plants are not set too far apart. The dark-green leaves are quite large compared with the previous species and form rosettes. The star-shaped, yellow flowers appear in loose clusters in June and July. There is also a cultivar with a coloured leaf, 'Variegatum.' Another good stonecrop for ground cover is *S. spurium* and its cultivars. This species grows between 10 and 20cm (4 and 8in) tall. It has creeping stems which root easily. The species itself has pink flowers from May to October. The cultivar 'Fuldaglut' has dark-red leaves and rose-pink flowers, while 'Dragon's Blood' has the same dark-red leaf and carmine pink flowers. 'Purple Carpet' is pink. There is again a cultivar 'Variegata.' There are many more attractive stonecrops. Look for them at a nursery that specializes in rock plants.

Sempervivum (houseleek)

Houseleeks are more suitable for small beds in the rock garden than for covering large areas among the usual perennials in the border. With their fleshy leaves they form attractive rosettes, which die off after flowering. By this time there are small rosettes on runners waiting to take over. The plant grows on roofs, walls, and stones, and likes a dry situation in the sun.

Silene (campion)

In the wild, *Silene* grows in sunny places on sandy, well-drained soil, which must nevertheless be fertile. There are

Detail of the flower of bunnies' ears, Stachys byzantina.

Comfrey, Symphytum grandiflorum, *is rather dull after the flowers die.*

a few rock plants, too, that can make ground cover in beds that are not too large.
S. uniflora (syn. *S. maritima*), especially 'Robin Whitebreast', is suitable for this. It reaches about 15cm (6 in), has pretty grey-green leaves, and nice white flowers in summer. These resemble those of the bladder campion. *S. shafta* is scarcely 10cm (4in) tall and has bright pink flowers from July to September.

Soleirolia (baby's tears)
This mossy little plant with the bright green leaves is grown as a house plant, but provided the winter is not too wet, forms a very low ground cover, which makes a lovely carpet where clumps of low-growing bulbs

such as cyclamen, scillas, and iris give colour and a contrast. The flowers of baby's tears can be ignored. The plant is still sometimes sold under its synonym *Helxine soleirolia*.

Stachys (bunnies' ears)
Bunnies' ears spreads by means of the prostrate stems which root readily. The stems and the leaves are covered in soft, grey hairs, hence the common name. *Stachys* likes fairly dry, humus-rich soil, and like other grey-leafed plants, plenty of sun. *S. byzantina* (formerly *S. lanata* or *S. olympia*), produces stems 40cm (16in) high, crowned with lilac-pink flowers that are partly hidden in the grey spikes. The plant then gives a general impression of being silver-grey.

The cultivar 'Silver Carpet', which rarely flowers, makes splendid ground cover, about 20cm (8in) high.

Symphytum (comfrey)
Comfrey is well known as a plant of wet places along rivers and by ponds. This species is not suitable for ground cover but the smaller, 30cm (12in), creeping species *Symphytum grandiflorum* is. It likes shade or half shade and damp, rich soil. The long-stemmed leaves form a carpet, with the pale-yellow flowers in small groups above them. The cultivar 'Wisley Blue' has pale blue flowers in April and May.

The greenish-yellow flowers of Tellima grandiflora.

Right: The tiny, variegated leaves of Thymus citriodorus *'Silver Posie.'*

Opposite page: Baby's tears, Soleirolia soleirolii, *makes good ground cover as well as an attractive house plant.*

Tellima

This lovely ground-cover plant will thrive even in the deepest shade, preferably in damp, humus-rich soil. It is closely related to *Tolmeia, Tiarella* and *Heuchera*. The leaves are very similar, and the leaves of *Tellima* are also pale green and hairy. Without the flower stem *Tellima* reaches 25cm (10in) while the flower stems, with the small flowers from April to July, will reach 50cm (20in). The name *T. grandiflora* suggests that the plant has large flowers but the opposite is true — they are small and only large compared with their relatives. Although the flowers are not striking, green with a very delicate red rim, the plant is attractive. The cultivar 'Rubra' has red leaves.

Thymus (thyme)

Apart from the scented culinary herb there are species of *Thymus* that have a creeping growth form and therefore make a good, very low ground cover.

The common *Thymus vulgaris*, the herb, is actually a shrub, so it does not belong here. The creeping thymes come under perennials or rock plants. There are various species and cultivars that are worth looking out for. Lemon thyme, *T. x citriodorus*, grows to about 15cm (6in) and has lilac-pink flowers in May and June. Most nurseries have only the golden-leafed cultivar 'Aureus' and the silver-grey 'Silver Queen' or 'Silver Posie' in their selection. *T. pseudo-lanuginosus*, the woolly thyme, is a pretty grey-leaved plant with

pink flowers that scarcely reaches 5cm (2in) in height. There are others that are popularly known as woolly thyme. The relationships of the genus *Thymus* are rather complicated for a non-expert. The creeping thyme, *T. serpyllum*, is a free-flowering species which, depending on the cultivar, has either white flowers, 'Albus', or deep red, 'Coccineus.'

Tiarella (foamflower)

The foamflower makes lovely ground cover in light shade and shade in damp, fertile soil. *Tiarella cordifolia* is a plant of damp woodland where it makes long runners and soon forms a beautiful, 20cm (8in) high, light-green carpet. The flower heads

stick out above this in April and May. *T. wherryi* produces no runners and reaches about 30cm (12in).

Tolmiea (pick-a-back plant)

Tolmiea is more often encountered in a flower shop, where it is sold as a house plant, than in a nursery specializing in perennials. Yet this pretty little plant with its softly-hairy, pale-green leaves does well in the garden and can spread vigorously there. During the summer a new plantlet forms in the centre of the leaf. When the leaf bends over to the ground on its long stalk, roots develop and a new plant is produced. *Tolmiea* likes cool, shady conditions, and normal, not too dry, soil. *T. menziesii* flowers in

May and June with long nodding spikes of tiny, greenish-brown flowers.

Trifolium (clover)

Clover will grow in sun and light shade in any soil. The wild clover is somewhat invasive but there is an attractive cultivar — *Trifolium repens* 'Penta-phyllum.' It has red-brown leaves with pretty markings and white flowers. It is only about 20cm (8in) high and flowers throughout the summer.

Tussilago (colt's-foot)

Colt's foot, *Tussilago farfara*, grows in the wild on roadside verges and on ploughed and fallow land. It produces yellow flowers in March. The leaf looks very like that of *Petasites alba*

although smaller. Because colt's-foot is common in the wild it is often overlooked as a garden plant. This 25cm (10in) high plant is suitable for large beds but needs to be kept under control.

Veronica (speedwell)

Among the speedwells there are plants that vary in size from 1.5m (5ft) down to 5cm (2in). They like a place in the sun or light shade, and well-drained soil. In many lawns, especially on sandy soil, the slender speedwell, *Veronica filiformis*, flowers abundantly. It makes a very pretty sight in May and June with its blue flowers. This 10cm (4in) high speedwell can be used as ground cover, although it must be kept within bounds.

Veronica austriaca *'Knallblau.'*

Above: The variegated periwinkle, Vinca major *'Variegata', makes a rather untidy ground cover.*

Right: The slender speedwell, Veronica filiformis.

Opposite page: The colt's-foot, Tussilago farfara.

The similar, though more compact and less invasive, *V. repens*, has light blue flowers and reaches 5cm (2in).
V. prostrata is a creeping species, 5 to 10cm (2 to 4in) high, that makes a nice edging or in-filling in the rock garden. It has violet-blue flowers in May and June, while the cultivar 'Alba' has white ones and 'Rosea' pink.
V. austriaca is striking during the flowering season, because the flower spikes — in various shades of blue according to the cultivar — almost totally hide the leaves. Some good cultivars are: 'Knallblau', 'Royal Blue', 'Shirley Blue', and 'Crater Lake Blue.'

Vinca (periwinkle)

Periwinkle is probably one of the best-known and most popular ground-cover plants. This is because it is evergreen and also very easy to grow. It is not fussy about soil provided this is not too poor or too dry, and it prefers shade or half shade.
Periwinkle can be planted in containers or allowed to grow over low walls with its long, decorative stems.
There are two species, *Vinca minor* and *V. major*, names which reflect their size. *V. minor* also occurs in the wild and forms long, trailing stems that root at the leaf nodes. The paired leaves are a shiny dark-green and the blue flowers appear above them in April and May which gives an attractive effect. There is a more free-flowering cultivar, 'Bowles Blue.'
The white-flowered cultivars are called 'Alba' and 'Gertrude Jekyll.' Besides those there is a reddish-purple form 'Atropurpurea', one with white on the leaves, 'Argentovariegata', and one with gold, 'Aureavariegata.'
V. major is larger in all respects. Whereas *V. minor* only reaches 10 to 15cm (4 to 6in), *V. major* grows to at least 40cm (16in). If the plants are set close together they will scramble over each other.
V. major also has blue flowers, with a hint of lilac.
'Reticulata' has leaves with yellow splashes, 'Variegata', white and green ones.

111

Viola labradorica *is worth planting for the foliage alone. It is pretty combined with baby's tears.*

Above: Viola sororia *'Albiflora', together with the yellow-flowered* Waldsteinia.

Left: Among the perennial violets there are many lovely cultivars such as this Viola cornuta *hybrid 'Vita.'*

Viola (violet)

There is a wide choice among the violets. The biennials are particularly well-known because they flower over a long period. There are perennials that are very attractive and have a long flowering season — the *Viola cornuta* hybrids. They are not really ground-cover plants because their growth form is too loose. Besides them there are some violets that do make good ground cover. They often have small flowers and a short flowering season but they are nice nevertheless.

One of the best known is the sweet violet, V. odorata, which is scented, as the name implies. It has velvety, mauve flowers in March and April. There is also a white cultivar, 'Alba', and a reddish-purple, 'Red Charm.' The plant grows to about 15cm (6in) and forms runners. It can tolerate a fair amount of shade and likes normal garden soil. Recently *V. labrodorica* has become very popular. It is a pretty, 10cm (4in) high ground-cover plant with an unusual purple shade to the leaf. It has mauve flowers in April and May. *V. sororia* 'Albiflora', too, makes good ground cover in sun or light shade. It has large leaves compared with the previous two violets. It reaches 15cm (4in) and in April and May produces white flowers. The cultivar 'Freckles' has white flowers, speckled with delicate purple. All these violets like normal garden soil that does not become too wet in winter.

Waldsteinia

This good, evergreen ground-cover plant for a fertile, somewhat acid, soil is satisfied with shade or half shade. The leaf of *Waldsteinia* is similar to that of a strawberry and the yellow flowers that appear in April are not unlike wild strawberry flowers. Indeed they both belong to the same family, the *Rosaceae*.
Waldsteinia geoides is about 20cm (8in) high and flowers in April and May. *W. ternata* has a creeping rootstock and is therefore more suitable for ground cover. It only reaches 10cm (4in) and has pretty yellow flowers in May and June.

112

The tall bracken Pteridium aquilinum *is native to woodland and moorland.*

Waldsteinia *makes pretty ground cover even without the flowers.*

Ferns

The number of ferns that are suitable for ground cover is not very large, but the few that are, are very attractive, and they are almost all plants for shady positions. Ferns have no flowers so it is the foliage that gives them their special character. That is often lovely — in some species it is deeply indented, in others it is evergreen. Both the variety of leaf forms and the spectacular emergence of new foliage in spring contribute to their value in the garden. What we call a leaf is a frond made up of a number of leaves or pinnae. Ferns generally multiply by underground runners, called rhizomes. The leaves which grow out of these determine the height of the plant. The common species are mentioned below. If you do become really interested there are other possibilities. It would then be best to go to a specialist nursery.

Adiantum (maidenhair)

The maidenhair ferns are very fragile, with delicate fronds, that can soon be damaged by the wind. They need to be planted in a sheltered spot. Only *Adiantum pedatum* and its cultivars are winter hardy in western Europe. They need to be planted in humus-rich, rather damp soil in the shade. The fronds are a lovely, bright green, about 25cm (10in) long, and develop throughout the summer. There are also cultivars such as 'Japonicum, and 'Aleuticum' — now more properly *A. pedatum* var. *subpumilum*. The rather shorter, deciduous *A. venustum* is amazingly hardy.

Gymnocarpium

These ferns make good ground cover for shaded areas. The names are rather confusing. For the non-expert it can be something of a problem. The oak fern, *Gymnocarpium dryopteris*, will tolerate some drought although it prefers damp, humus-rich soil. The fronds are about 40cm (16in) long. It is suitable for planting under trees and shrubs. The limestone fern, *G. robertianum* syn. *Thelypteris robertianum*, is a native of limestone areas, so it grows well in lime-rich soil and on walls. It reaches about 50cm (20in).

113

Onoclea (sensitive fern)

This lovely fern, with its bright-green, almost triangular and deeply-incised fronds, reaches 50 to 70cm (20 to 28in). In summer little brown balls containing the spores develop on the fronds. *Onoclea sensibilis* is happiest in damp, humus-rich soil, in light shade. It will grow in the sun, provided the soil is damp enough, for example in a bog. It is fairly sensitive to wind and frost.

Polypodium (polypody)

There are actually very few ferns suitable for ground-cover in deep shade.
Polypody, *Polypodium vulgare*, and intermediate polypody, *P. interjectum*, are very much at home here. They occur in the wild on rocks, walls and tree trunks although *P. interjectum* is more shade- and lime-loving. *P. vulgare* has fronds about 15cm (6in) long, which survive even quite severe frosts. The new leaves unroll quite late, sometimes not until June. *P. interjectum* is taller, about 40cm (16in), and the fronds are only 15cm (6in) broad, which give it a more delicate appearance. It likes a damper soil, with more humus than the polypody.

Pteridium (bracken)

Bracken, *Pteridium aquilinum*, covers large tracts of ground in woodland and open ground. Although it looks attractive, with pale green fronds in spring and good autumn colours, it should on no account be introduced into a garden, even a large one, since it is almost impossible to control.

Thelypteris (marsh fern and beech fern)

The marsh fern, *Thelypteris palustris* (syn. *T. thelypteroides*) grows to about 60cm (24in) and has pretty, light-green foliage. It is at home on marshy to very wet ground, but will also tolerate a fair amount of drought. The wetter the ground the more sun it can stand. The beech fern, *Phegopteris connectilis* (syn. *Thelypteris phegopteris*), has darker green, slightly hairy fronds that stand high up on the brownish stalks and reach about 40cm (16in). It makes good ground cover, even for a small

garden, preferring damp, humus-rich soil. In the wild it also grows under beech trees and shrubs. That shows that it is suitable for shade and half shade. It must not be planted in deep shade.

Grasses

Apart from the grasses used for lawns that are to be walked on and played on, and the more succulent meadow grasses, there is a number of ornamental grasses suitable for filling large or small beds. Generally speaking these are taller and coarser than the grasses in a lawn mixture. They are not mown, so they are not suitable for walking on.

The structure of grasses, with a tall, narrow leaf, makes a nice contrast with many other plants, particularly if the leaf is very delicate or very large. Grasses in flower, too, make a nice impression among perennials and shrubs.

There are tussock-forming grasses that need to be planted close together to give good cover.

There are other grasses that produce rhizomes and in time make thick mats.

Carex (sedge)

The lower-growing species of sedge make good ground cover in sun and light shade and the odd one is suitable for a more shaded situation. *Carex morrowii* (syn. *C. oshimensis*) 'Variegata' is a variegated, evergreen sedge with long,

The variegated Carex murrowii 'Variegata.'

Opposite page: The periwinkle, Vinca major.

narrow leaves that forms dense tussocks. It likes light shade and is not fussy about the soil. This decorative plant flowers in April and May. Apart from this cultivar there is also 'Evergold.' *C. plantaginea* is a pretty, broad-leaved sedge for shade, with tiny flowers.

Festuca (fescue)

This grass needs dry soil and sun to light shade. *Festuca gautieri*, formerly *S. scoparia*, makes a good, green sward about 30cm (12in) high with flowers from May to July. *F. glauca*, blue fescue, has pretty, very fine, grey-

Koeleria glauca *makes nice ground cover but also looks good as a specimen plant on sandy soil.*

The white Luzula nivea *is lovely when in flower.*

green leaves about the same height. It flowers in May and June.

Koeleria (hair grass)

Koeleria glauca is a pretty, grey-blue grass that forms a flat turf, no more than 30cm (12in) high. It needs a position in the sun in well-drained, dry soil.

Luzula (woodrush)

Woodrushes are green throughout the winter, which is useful because then the garden can lack green for a long time. The woodrush prefers shade and half shade and humus-rich soil. The most usual species are *Luzula nivea*, the snowy woodrush, 40cm (16in) tall with striking white flowers in June and July, *L. pilosa*, the same

height, with green leaves, for damp but not wet soil. *L. sylvatica*, also 40cm (16in), has light green leaves. There is also a variegated cultivar, 'Marginata.'

Phalaris (Canary grass)

Phalaris arundinacea 'Picta', sometimes called "gardener's garters", is a very invasive grass. The leaf is striped and the more sun the plant receives the whiter the stripes become. The stems with the leaves grow to 50cm (20in), and with the flowers the plant reaches about 80cm (32in). It can grow in dry as well as wet places.

Bamboos

The number of bamboos suitable for ground cover is very small. Bamboos are in general very invasive and difficult to keep in check. If you want to keep them in their place it is advisable to bury a sheet of corrugated plastic round them to a depth of at least a metre.

If a root does escape the cordon it must be cut off immediately to prevent the plant taking hold. Suitable species are the 30cm (12in) high *Pleioblastus pygmaeus*, *Shibatea kumasasa* (50cm) (20in), and *Sasa veitchii* (50cm) (20in). The last has quite broad leaves that have a white edge in the winter. In general, bamboos like damp, fertile, open soil, and a position in sun or half shade.

Sasa veitchii *has a white rim to the leaf in winter.*

Right: The splendid flower of Mesembryanthemum criniflorum *opens only when the sun is shining.*

Above: The daisy-like flowers of the annual fleabane, Erigeron karvinskianus.

Annuals

There are some annuals that form a colourful carpet in the summer. These plants, that mostly die off at the first frosts, are suitable for planting among roses and in the border. The best time to plant them, since they are tender, is after mid-May, when the last night frosts should be past. The following list contains those annuals that are usually used as ground cover. Most of them like sun and normal, garden soil.

Brachycome iberidifolia

This is a pretty, branching, plant about 30cm (12in) high, with daisy-like flowers. The most usual one has bright blue flowers, but there are also white and pink forms.

Erigeron (fleabane)

The delicate white to pink flowers of this annual look like small daisies.

The stems are thin and the leaves tiny. In full sun on dry soil *Erigeron karvinskianus* (syn. *E. mucronatus*), will flower the whole summer and set seed.

In mild winters much of the seed will survive so you can expect an explosion of new plants all over the garden. Some people regard it as a weed, but after all, there are many pretty weeds.

Gazania splendens

This annual has prostrate stems and covers the ground beautifully. It is a true sun lover. There are various colours and

shades from creamy white to warm orange.

Gazania rigens var. *uniflora* has yellow or orange yellow flowers with white spots in the centre.

Impatiens walleriana (busy Lizzie)

This plant will also tolerate half shade and is useful if only for that. It grows to about 40cm (16in) and flowers in a range of colours from white to deep pink, orange or purple.

Limnanthes douglasii (poached egg plant)

The yellow flowers with the white border give the plant its name. It is a fast-growing annual, about 20cm (8in) high, in flower from June to

Detail of the unusual flower of the mignonette, Reseda odorata.

The bright yellow and white flowers of the poached egg plant, Limnanthes douglasii.

September. The fragrant flowers are much visited by bees.

Lobelia erinus

There are now pink- and carmine red-flowering varieties of this predominantly blue annual.
It can stand some shade and fairly damp soil.

Lobularia maritima (sweet alyssum)

Lobularia maritima (syn. *Alyssum maritimum*), grows to 10cm (4in)and has small white, pink, or mauve flowers. If you cut off the dead flowers there will be a second crop.
Sweet alyssum seeds freely and can spring up in the most unexpected places next year.
It prefers dry soil.

Mesembryanthemum (Livingstone daisy)

This is a prostrate, succulent plant about 10cm (4in) high, with pearly hairs on leaves and stems.
Mesembryanthemum criniflorum (syn. *Dorotheanthus bellidiformis*), has striking, daisy-like flowers, in soft shades or bright colours. It likes sun and dry ground and will thrive in quite poor soil.

Persicaria capitata

Persicaria capitata (syn. *Polygonum capitatum*), can overwinter provided the weather is not too severe. It has prostrate stalks and spherical heads of pink flowers. It can tolerate some shade and is not fussy about the soil.

Reseda odorata (mignonette)

Mignonette grows to 40cm (16in) and produces bunches of yellow-green flowers, which have a delicious scent. It is useful as a cut flower and is also a good bee plant.

Sanvitalia procumbens (creeping zinnia)

This makes nice ground cover with its prostrate stems. It has yellow flowers with a dark centre. Plant it in the sun for really exuberant flowering, although it will grow in light shade.

Senecio bicolor

Although it is not a true ground-cover plant this is pretty for filling beds. The attraction lies in the silver-grey foliage.

Violets can self-seed everywhere, even among the plants in the vegetable garden. Above: Polygonum capitatum *can survive mild winters.*

Right: The annual Lobularia maritima, *sweet alyssum, can spread by seed.*

If it is protected from severe frosts it will overwinter and produce clusters of yellow flowers in the second year. It likes a situation in dry soil.

Silene pendula (nodding catchfly)

This 25cm (10in) high plant can be bought in early spring or raised from seed. It flowers in spring and early summer. It is not fussy about the soil provided it is not too damp. Flowers are usually red, but there are cultivars available with white, salmon-pink, dark crimson, or red flowers. There are single and double forms.

Tropaeolum majus (nasturtium)

Although better known as a climber, the nasturtium can be used for ground cover. There are both climbing and compact varieties.

The flower colour varies from pale yellow to deep orange, and there are also forms with red or variegated leaves.

The more unusual ones you will have to grow from seed yourself or go to a nursery specializing in annuals.

Viola (pansy)

There are many violets that are nice for filling large beds. Recently, as well as the large-flowered pansies, pretty small ones have come onto the market, in various colours such as pale yellow, yellow, blue, and mauve.

There is also the *Viola tricolor,* or heartsease, that is, as the Latin name implies, three coloured, purple, yellow, and gold.

Corydalis solida, *bird-in-a-bush.*
Left: The yellow anemone, Anemone
ranunculoides, *prefers a light place in
woodland.*
Previous page: Sanvitalia procumbens, *the
creeping zinnia, makes a lively carpet of
yellow flowers in the sun.*

Bulbs, tubers, and rhizomatous plants

The foliage of bulbs, tubers, and rhizomatous plants usually dies off soon after flowering, which means it only provides temporary ground cover. It is not advisable, therefore, to fill large beds with them. They can be useful if the beds contain other plants, or where shrubs are going to come into leaf and become a feature in their place. Most bulbs, tubers, and rhizomatous plants are planted in the autumn. Exceptions to this are mentioned in the descriptions.

Allium ursinum (ramsons)

There is a wide variety of ornamental onion available, ranging in height from 20cm to a good 1.5m (8in to 5ft). Ramsons is the most suitable for larger beds and usually does not exceed 20cm (8in).

In the wild it grows in woodlands where it gives off a strong smell of onions. In spring it has clusters of white, star-shaped flowers.

The plant likes damp, humus-rich soil and light shade.

Anemone

The blue anemone, *Anemone blanda*, does not need to be blue — there are white forms including the lovely 'White Splendour' as well as pink ones. This 10cm (4in) high anemone likes sun to light shade in normal, preferably humus-rich soil. It flowers in March and April.

The wood anemone, *A. nemorosa*, flowers at the same time. It is about the same height as *A. blanda*, but the flowers are smaller and have fewer petals. It is a lovely plant to allow to naturalize under trees and among shrubs. There is a double cultivar, 'Alba Plena', and a beautiful soft, lilac-blue one, 'Robinsoniana', slightly taller with larger and more spectacular flowers.

The yellow anemone, *A. ranunculoides*, looks not unlike the wood anemone and has the same requirements. None of the anemones can stand having their rootstocks dry out, and they must be planted as soon as they arrive.

The hardy cyclamen, Cyclamen hederifolium, *flowers in September.*

Above: The winter aconite, Eranthis, *is one of the earliest plants to flower.*
Right: The lesser celandine, Ranunculus ficaria, *grows in the wild.*

Corydalis

In the wild, *Corydalis solida* grows in woodland and under shrubs. It likes humus-rich, fairly damp soil, and light shade. The light-green leaves are deeply cut, so they resemble ferns. This nice little plant flowers in March and April with bunches of lilac-pink tubular flowers. *C. cava* has rather larger flowers.

Cyclamen (wild cyclamen)

There are some small-flowered cyclamen that are suitable for naturalizing. They have large, flat corms and grow best under shrubs, where they lend themselves well to edging along hedges.
Cyclamen coum does not exceed 15cm (6in) and early in the year, sometimes even in

January, has tiny, pink flowers. It likes humus-rich, fertile, and fairly loose soil. It is a good idea to cover the corms with fallen leaves in winter.
C. purpurascens flowers in August to September, with its crimson flowers sticking up above the leaves. Like the autumn-flowering
C. hederafolium, it needs fertile, humus-rich soil in light shade. The latter species also has pink flowers, but there is a nice white cultivar, 'Alba.'
These cyclamen also appreciate some protection during hard frost.
C. hederafolium flowers in September and October, after which the attractive, ivy-shaped leaf develops that dies off in spring.

Eranthis (winter aconite)

The winter aconite has golden yellow flowers in February and March. They are surrounded by a frill of deeply-indented, bright-green leaves. *Eranthis x cilicica* and *E. hyemalis* prefer light shade and normal, not too dry, soil.

Oxalis (wood sorrel)

There are many species of sorrel, one of which, *Oxalis acetosella*, has been described under perennials. *O. adenophylla* has pretty, blue-green leaves that consist of heart-shaped leaflets. Depending on the weather conditions they are open or folded shut. The flowers are lilac-pink and appear in May and June. The whole plant grows no higher than 7cm (3in).

It is not so suitable for large beds, but goes well in the rock garden.

Ranunculus ficaria (lesser celandine)

Although this little plant is often regarded as a weed, because it can spread very rapidly through its white tubers, it does make attractive ground cover.
It grows best in shaded, damp situations. It flowers as early as February or March and has bright yellow, buttercup-like flowers. It is very low-growing. It is not usually available for sale because it is so common but there are nurseries that specialize in it.
There are about a hundred different forms in the British national collection.

Shrubs

Generally speaking, shrubs are suitable as ground cover only for large beds, because one specimen can cover a considerable area. This does not, however, apply to the low-growing *Ericaeae*, the heather family. These are small in comparison with other woody species.

Arctostaphylos (bearberry)

Arctostaphylos uva-ursi belongs to the heather family and forms a very low, creeping, evergreen shrub. The small leaves are a shiny dark green. In April and May it has pink and white flowers, followed by red berries. It likes peaty, dry soil and a sunny position, with some shelter.

Berberis (barberry)

Most of the barberries are upright shrubs, but some lower species are used as ground cover for large areas. The twigs have very sharp thorns, which make pruning an unpleasant task. There are both evergreen and deciduous species. Some cultivars have very striking flowers that hang in bunches on the twigs, followed by colourful fruits. The barberry is not fussy about soil type, but the most suitable is fertile sandy soil. It likes sun to light shade. Several cultivars of the deciduous *Berberis thunbergii* make good cover, for example 'Carpetbagger', with spreading branches and bright-green leaves, and 'Green Carpet', a barberry with a very flat growth

The prostrate Cotoneaster dammeri
'Major.'
Right: The brilliant blossom of the
flowering quince, Chaenomeles x superba
'Cameo.'
Above: The herringbone pattern of the
branches is very obvious in this
Cotoneaster horizontalis.

form that has red berries that stand out against the leaves.

Calluna (heather)

Various cultivars of heather have a prostrate form and are therefore used for ground cover. These are suitable for a special heather garden or for combining with rhododendrons or azaleas, but not for planting with perennials that grow and flower luxuriantly. There is only one species, *Calluna vulgaris*, but there are dozens of cultivars, among them ones with green, grey, or variegated leaves. The flowers vary in colour from white through pink to red and purple. Heathers need acid soil and sun or light shade. The plants must be clipped after flowering to keep the plants tidy. The flowering season varies according to the cultivar but ranges from June to December.

Chaenomeles (flowering quince)

The flowering quince is suitable only for large areas and is often used in parks and other public open spaces. It makes a large, thorny shrub with beautiful, waxy flowers in white, pink, orange, and many shades of red. Most cultivars flower early, in March or April. The green or yellow fruits that follow the flowers have a very unusual scent.
The shrub flowers on old wood so pruning has to be done as lightly as possible.
Good cultivars for ground cover include the bright orange *Chaenomeles japonica* 'Sargentii', the red *C. x superba* 'Rowallane', the white-flowering 'Jet Trail', the deep scarlet 'Nicoline', and the almost thornless, red 'Texas Scarlet.' The flowering quince likes fertile, well-drained soil and a sunny position, although it can stand light shade.

Cotoneaster

Ground-covering cotoneasters are not very decorative, but the red fruits give a splash of colour in the autumn. In private gardens this shrub is most suitable for underplanting among large groups of shrubs, or for using on slopes. There are both evergreen and deciduous species.

125

The evergreen species *Cotoneaster dammeri* and *C. microphyllus* and several of their cultivars form good, low-growing shrubs which will grow in sun or half shade, preferably in fertile, sandy soil. Both species have tiny, dark-green leaves, in the case of the latter with a grey, felty underside. The white flowers are followed by a few red berries. The most suitable for gardens is the deciduous *C. horizontalis*, because in the autumn the fish-bone pattern of stiff branches is covered in red berries. It is also suitable for training against a wall.

Cytisus (broom)

Broom always calls up a picture of the yellow shrub with branches like a witch's broom that provides a riot of colour along roadside verges. This is certainly no ground-cover plant. Brooms like light, sandy soil and a sunny situation.

It is advisable to prune them after flowering, otherwise the underside will become brown after several seasons and the shrub will outgrow its strength.

Cytisus decumbens only reaches 20cm (8in) in height, is covered in golden-yellow flowers in May and June, and is one of the prettiest and most hardy ground-cover species.

C. x kewensis, too, is creeping, grows to 30cm (12in) high and a good 1.5m (5ft) wide.

In May it has sulphur-yellow to creamy-white flowers.

C. purpureus (syn. *Chamae-cytisus purpureus*) 'Atropurpureus' becomes rather taller, but still has a prostrate growth form, which makes it suitable for planting on slopes. It has countless purple flowers in May and June.

Empetrum (crowberry)

The little shrub, *Empetrum nigrum*, is native to peaty and boggy moors in Great Britain and therefore a neighbour of the heather. It can be planted in a heather garden. It needs peaty, acid soil in sun to half shade. The flowers and berries are not particularly striking.

Erica (heath)

Of the 600 or so species of heath several are native to the British

The golden-leafed Euonymus fortunei *'Emerald 'n' Gold.'*

Opposite page: The small flowers of the wintergreen, Gaultheria shallon, *stand out well against the leathery, dark green leaves.*

Isles, including *Erica tetralix*, the cross-leaved heath. *E. ciliaris*, the Dorset heath, is a rarity, but *E. cinerea*, bell heather, is more common. Among the cultivars there is a wide variation in flowering season so that it is possible to have some colour in the heather garden almost all the year round. Like *Calluna, Erica* is also suitable for a garden with acid-loving plants, such as rhododendrons. The heaths like peaty, fertile, soil, in sun or half shade.

Euonymus

This family includes the spindle, a tall shrub that has beautiful pink berries with orange seeds. The species that is suitable for ground cover, *Euonymus fortunei* with its cultivars, is evergreen. The oval leaves vary in colour from bright- or dark-green to silver or gold variegated ones. As well as being used for ground cover, this shrub also climbs if planted against a wall or tree trunk. It is not fussy about soil and will grow in any good garden soil. It prefers sun or half shade. Not all species flower freely but that is really no loss as it is the foliage that is attractive, although the seeds are pretty. When you are buying a plant ask if it sets seed — most of the variegated ones do not.

Gaultheria (wintergreen)

Gaultheria procumbens likes very humus-rich, somewhat acid soil and therefore can be planted with bell heather, to which it is related. Wintergreen, with its red berries, is often sold as a house plant at Christmas time. The low humidity soon causes the leaves to droop. Put the plant some-where cool if the weather is frosty, or plant in the garden. It is seen to best advantage in a big group. This attractive little plant grows to no more than 15cm (6in) and has shiny, leathery leaves that turn brown in winter. The branches of *G. shallon* are sold as foliage in flower shops. This species has leathery leaves on 80cm (32in) long branches. It can tolerate more shade and thrives very well in sandy soil.

Genista (greenweeds)

The *Genistas* are also commonly known as broom, and resemble the *Cytisus* in flower and growth habit.

The honeysuckle, Lonicera periclymenum *'Serotina', makes lovely ground cover.*

Right: The greenweed, Genista sagittalis, *flowers freely in suitable conditions.*

Previous page: Rose of Sharon, Hypericum calycinum, *is especially suitable for filling large beds.*

Only a few of them are suitable for ground cover. They prefer a position in full sun on poor, sandy soil, which does not become too wet in the winter. *Genista pilosa* forms a prostrate to creeping shrub about 40cm (16in) high, with yellow flowers in May and June, and a second flowering in the autumn. The branches, fruits, and the underside of the leaves have fine hairs on them. This species is hardy and a native plant in western Europe. *G. sagittalis* has tangled, winged, green, prostrate stems that form a good, evergreen carpet 10 to 20cm (4 to 8in) high. *G. tinctoria*, dyers greenweed, grows upward. Its cultivar 'Golden Plate', in contrast, forms a creeping, spreading shrub no more than 30cm (12in) high. This also has yellow flowers in late June and early July. This is not on recent lists from nurseries.

Hypericum (rose of Sharon)

The best ground-cover plant among these species is *Hypericum calycinum*, which has vigorous underground runners. The 8cm (3in) long leaves stay on the plant well into the winter. They only turn rather brown in the early spring. Cut them off, so that the young, green foliage has space to develop.

The saucer-shaped, deep-yellow flowers have a cluster of stamens in the centre. The season is July to September.

This shrub prefers light shade, and any good garden soil is suitable, provided it is well drained.

Lonicera

This family includes the honeysuckle, the deliciously scented climber. There are, however, two evergreen shrubs suitable for ground cover, *Lonicera nitida* and *L. pileata*. They are only appropriate only for large beds and slopes. Both have delicate leaves and not very striking flowers. *L. nitida* has shiny, mauve berries. This shrub grows to about 1m (3ft) high, *L. piliata* about 60cm (24in). They will grow in sun or light shade. They are not fussy about the soil as long as it is not too dry or too poor.

Mahonia

The low *Mahonias* are very suitable for planting in large groups. They form a nice contrast to other plants with their pretty leaves that, in some species, turn bronze in the winter. If *M. aquifolium* is cut back after flowering it remains compact. It can grow in full sun, but prefers light shade. Humus-rich soil is recommended. Nice cultivars are the 60cm (24in) high 'Apollo' with long stems of deep, golden-yellow flowers in May, and 'Atropurpurea', a similar height, with dark-green leaves that become dark bronze-red in winter.

Rubus (bramble)

The bramble is such an invasive plant that you would probably rather not see it in your garden. There are, however, some species that are suitable for covering large beds and slopes, but they are not advisable for small gardens. Brambles will grow in any, preferably fertile, soil, in sun or light shade. *Rubus arcticus* has a creeping rootstock and grows to 20cm (8in). The leaves have three leaflets. In June the shrub bears 2cm (1in) diameter flowers, after which the edible, brownish-yellow fruits appear. There are several good cultivars. The twigs of the evergreen *R. calycinoides* (syn. *R. pentalobus)*, which root at the nodes, only reach 10cm (4in) in height. The almost round, shiny leaves are grey beneath. There are white flowers in May and June, followed by bright red fruit. This species likes damp soil and some shade. *R. fruticosus* contains several good cultivars for ground cover in large beds, for example 'Dart's Robertville', that is semi-evergreen. It does not flower very well, so the fruits are scarce. The evergreen *R. tricolor* is very attractive, with heart-shaped, dark-green leaves that have a white felt underneath. It has white flowers in July, followed sometimes by edible red fruit. 'Dart's Evergreen' has more shiny leaves.

Salix (willow)

Most willows grow into trees or large shrubs but there are a few species that do not grow tall, and even one creeping species, *Salix repens*. This 1m (3ft) high shrub,

Various spireas are suitable for making large blocks of colour.

Right: Gorse, Ulex europaeus, *has stout, thorny branches. In the season these are covered in deep yellow pea flowers.*

Opposite page: The bramble, Rubus, *is most suitable for rather rough planting.*

with its prostrate, brown twigs has fairly small leaves that are often hairy beneath, which give a soft to grey-green impression. It produces catkins in April, likes dry ground, and is therefore suitable for slopes. There are a couple of nice cultivars with grey, more hairy leaves. The creeping willow can grow in sun or light shade.

Spiraea

Spiraea, not to be confused with the perennial *Astilbe*, has various forms.
The most suitable for ground cover is *S. decumbens*, a 25cm (10in) high and 40cm (16in) broad shrub with leaves 3cm (1in) long. In June flat flower heads appear with tiny white flowers.
S. japonica has several low cultivars which make nice cover, provided they are planted close together. 'Alpina', for instance, only reaches 35cm (14in) and has round clumps of pink flowers in June and July. 'Bullata' has rose-pink flowers in July and is taller at 40cm (16in). Very attractive, but rather taller, at 80cm (32in), is 'Shirobana'. The nice thing about this form is that there are white and pink flowers on the same bush. *Spiraea* likes a sunny position, but is not fussy about the soil — ordinary garden soil will do.

Ulex (gorse)

The gorse, *Ulex europaeus*, a native of western Europe, is thickly covered with stiff spines. It is a relative of the brooms, which is obvious from the flowers which appear in April and May. It grows to 1.5m (5ft) in height and is not completely hardy.

Vaccinium (cowberry, billberry)

The cowberry, *Vaccinium vitis-idaea* and its cultivars, is a native of western Europe that is suitable for ground cover.
It keeps its leaves in winter. The bilberry, *V. myrtillus*, is, in contrast, deciduous. Both species produce edible berries, the former red, the latter blue to black. The cowberry, with its leathery green leaves, makes a nice, creeping shrub about 30cm (12in) high. The bilberry is more

131

The various species of ivy Hedera helix *and* H. hibernica *make outstanding ground cover.*
Left: The variegated cultivar of ivy 'Aureovariegata' *makes a lovely smooth carpet.*
Opposite page: 'Apollo' is a beautiful, low-growing cultivar of Mahonia aquifolium.
Previous page: The rock rose, Helianthemum.

upright and less suitable for ground cover because it has quite a loose growth form. It does, however, produce a thick carpet with its spreading roots after several years, so excluding other plants. Both species are related to the heathers so are suitable for a heather garden or under a group of rhododendrons and azaleas.

The shrubs prefer half shade in humus-rich acid soil.

Climbing plants

If a climbing plant cannot find any support it will grow along the ground. This does not mean that all climbing plants are suitable for ground cover, because some are too wild or too delicate. The ones listed below are suitable.

Hedera (ivy)

Ivy is a very well-known evergreen ground-cover plant. For a small garden choose a small-leafed cultivar, such as *Hedera helix* 'Baltica', or 'Pittsburgh.' Larger gardens and slopes can be planted with large-leafed ones, which often have longer stems than the smaller ones. Good large-leafed ones are *H. helix* 'Woener', and the Irish ivy, *H. hibernica*. The green-leafed ivies will tolerate a lot of shade, but also more sun. In that case the soil must be sufficiently damp. The variegated forms are not so robust and do not do well in deep shade. Although ivy is not too fussy about soil it thrives best in damp, humus-rich, fertile soil. *H. colchica* has larger, more elliptical to round leaves.

There are shrub forms of both *H. helix* and *H. colchica*. These are compact and arise from cuttings of non-climbing shoots.

Hydrangea (climbing hydrangea)

The climbing hydrangea, *Hydrangea petiolaris*, is a well-known deciduous wall-shrub with pretty, brown twigs and flat heads of white flowers in June and July. These turn brown and remain as a lacy decoration through the winter.

The climbing hydrangea is very good for filling large beds in sun or shade. It prefers humus-rich, damp soil.

Lonicera (honeysuckle)

Apart from the shrub honey-suckles already mentioned there

are a number of lovely climbing plants that make good ground cover. You will appreciate that because of their vigour they are suitable only for large beds and slopes. They like humus-rich soil, in either sun or half shade, although the flowers will be less prolific out of the sun. The honeysuckle has a delicious scent, especially in the evening, and it attracts many insects. The evergreen *Lonicera japonica* has some good cultivars that are suitable, among others 'Dart's World', with scented, white flowers that age to yellow, in June to September, and 'Hall's Prolific', also white to yellow. Both of these have black berries. *L. henryi* is also evergreen. It is a pity that the flowers are not

more striking. The yellowish-white flowers, about 2cm (1in) long, come out in pairs from July to September. The berries are blue-black.

More familiar is the native honeysuckle that grows wild in woods, *L. periclymenum*. The cream to mauve flowers grow in bunches in June to August and smell beautiful. They are followed by red berries. There are several nice cultivars, including 'Belgica Select', free-flowering with cream flowers that are tinged with mauve on the outside.

This is an improved form of 'Belgica.' 'Serotina' is a lovely cultivar, with flowers that are dark purple outside and pale yellow on the inside.

This often has a somewhat slow

start, but once it does get established it will thrive. It makes good ground cover and can be planted in association with sturdy, ground-covering shrubs, such as some of the cotoneasters, that are rather dull and hardly flower.

Parthenocissus (Virginia creeper)

The Virginia creeper is a deciduous climber that attaches itself to surfaces and so makes it way upwards. It is attractive on account of its lovely autumn colours. Walls are transformed suddenly into curtains of beautiful yellow, orange, and deep red. The flowers are insignificant.

It is suitable for ground cover, but for large areas only, such as

slopes. It is happy in normal garden soil in sun or half shade. *Parthenocissus quinquifolia* has five leaflets, as the name suggests. The cultivar 'Engelmannii' is the most usual one. This is a more delicate cultivar. The leaf of *P. tricuspidata* begins in threes, but higher up it has entire, lobed leaves. There are good cultivars available.

Wisteria

Wisteria, too, can be used as ground cover, and with its twisted, gnarled stems, it can form a wild, undulating surface. You need to keep in mind that this is a plant suitable only for large areas and slopes. In May, just before the leaves appear, *Wisteria* produces white, lilac-blue or lilac-pink sprays of flowers, depending on the cultivar.
The best species for ground cover is *W. sinensis*.
It likes sun to light shade and normal, fertile soil.

Roses

There is a huge choice among roses. It includes a number of good, low-growing, ground-covering shrubs. A few of these, planted in a bed of ground-covering perennials can look very pretty. They also show themselves to be very valuable because many of them will go on flowering throughout the summer.
Roses prefer fertile soil that is certainly not wet. Standing water can be fatal for them.

They need regular feeding, but less often if the ground is heavy. On heavy clay you will need to dig in peat or compost.
On light, rather acid, sandy soil you will need to add fertilizer and compost to the soil. Roses do very well in peat, provided it is not too acid.
It is advisable to use special rose fertilizer and apply it well round the roses. Never plant roses where water can drip in them from trees or roofs and ensure that they have at least four hours of sun each day. That will not always happen in this climate but roses do need a lot of light. Do not plant them in too confined a place, but choose a more open position.
The relative humidity should not be at a high level, because that

encourages diseases such as mildew and black spot. Below there are some suggestions for suitable roses. They are divided into those that flower throughout the season, remontant roses, and those that flower only once.

Remontant cultivars

Rosa 'Eyeopener', blood-red with a bundle of yellow stamens in the centre, 'Nozomi', with flat, single, blush-pink flowers, and 'White Carpet.' Other white cultivars are 'Snowball', 'Snow Carpet', and 'Swany.'

Roses flowering once

There are roses with a more natural character such as the pink *Rosa arvensis*, the bright pink 'Max Graf', the 'White Max Graf', the 'Red Max Graf', and the white cultivar 'Paulii Alba.' The pink-flowering 'Pink Spray' has a more cultivated look, as has the rather taller 'White Spray', which does sometimes produce a second crop of flowers, especially if the dead heads are removed.

Climbing roses

The pale-pink 'New Dawn' is suitable for large beds and slopes. Specialist rose growers will be able to recommend other suitable cultivars because there are many.

It is possible to mention only a very small selection here.

Among the junipers there are several species and cultivars suitable for ground cover, such as Juniperus sabina *'Broadmoor.'*

Conifers

Conifers are very attractive for many people because they are evergreen. Do not use too many different species and cultivars because that will make the garden look flat and uninteresting. There are good, ground-covering conifers, which provided they are not used on too large a scale, and are combined with suitable plants and shrubs, for example with heathers, will provide contrast in the garden.

Most ground-covering conifers belong to the genus *Juniperus*.

Juniperus (juniper)

Among the junipers there are both upright and prostrate forms. Most species like poor sandy soil and sun to light shade. The common juniper, *Juniperus communis*, has several prostrate cultivars such as 'Hornibrookii', and 'Repanda.'

The name of *J. horizontalis* indicates its growth form, which is strongly horizontal. Further ground-cover cultivars are the silver-blue-grey 'Blue Chip', the dark grey-green 'Emerald Spreader', the silver-blue 'Jade River', the green 'Prince of Wales', which has a purplish sheen in the winter, the green to blue-green 'Prostrata', and the bright silver-blue 'Wiltonii.' The last is particularly attractive.

Various cultivars of *J. sabina* are also useful, such as the soft-green 'Broadmoor', the green to grey-green 'Tam No Blight', which reaches 50cm (20in), and the very low, dark-green 'Thomsen.'

The last in the series is *J. squamata* 'Blue Carpet', a beautiful blue-grey cultivar with flat, spreading branches and a fairly close growth habit.

Microbiota

This unusual ground-covering conifer has bright-green foliage that becomes a lovely purple in winter. There is only one species, *Microbiota decussata*.

Taxus (yew)

For large beds and for slopes the 50cm (20in) high *Taxus baccata* 'Repandens', with its dark-green leaves, is very suitable. The yew is one of the few conifers that can easily be combined with all kinds of woody shrubs, and is not out of place in the herbaceous border either. It can grow in sun or shade and is not fussy about the soil, provided it is not too poor.

Bibliography

Index Hortensis, Vol 1, Perennials
Piers Trehane (ed.), Quarterjack Publishing, Wimborne,
Dorset.

New Flora of the British Isles,
Clive Stace, Cambridge University Press, Cambridge.

Plants for Ground-Cover,
G. S. Thomas, Dent & Sons, London/Melbourne.

The RHS Gardeners' Encyclopedia of Plants,
Christopher Brickhill (ed.) , Dorling Kindersley, London/New
York/Stuttgart.

The RHS Plant Finder 1996/97 Edition,
Tony Lloyd (ed.), Moorland Publishing Company, Ashbourne,
Derbyshire.

Wyman's Gardening Encyclopedia,
Donald Wyman, The Macmillan Company, New York.

Useful addresses

In Great Britain:

Names and addresses of specialist nurseries are listed in the
RHS Plant Finder.

For inquiries on all aspects of gardening, including the details
of the annual Chelsea Flower Show, contact:
The Royal Horticultural Society
80 Vincent Square
London SW1P 2PE

In the United States:

The American Horticultural Society
Box 0105
Mount Vernon
Virginia 22121

The Massachusetts Horticultural Society
300 Massachusetts Avenue
Boston
Massachusetts 2115

The Pacific Horticultural Foundation
Box 485
Berkeley
California 94941

Photo credits

M. Kurpershoek, Amsterdam: title page, pages 10 below, 11, 13, 15, 18 left, 19, 22, 25, 26 below, 28, 29, 30, 31, 32, 34, 36, 39, 40, 43, 45 left, 51 below, 57, 59, 60, 61, 65, 70, 71 right, 72, 73, 74 below right, 75, 76, 77, 78 left and below right, 79 left, 80 right, 81 left, 82, 83 left, 84, 85 left, 86 below right, 88, 90 left and below right, 91 below left, 92, 93 above left and right, 95, 98, 99 left, 100 right, 101, 102, 103 above left, 104, 105 left, 106 right, 107 left, 108, 109 left, 112 above right, 113 left, 114, 115, 116, 117 left, 118, 119 right and above left, 120, 121, 122, 123 below left, 131, 136, 139.

G. Otter, IJsselstein: pages 6, 7, 8 right, 9, 10 above, 12, 14, 16, 17, 18 right, 20, 21, 23, 24, 26 above, 27, 33, 35, 37, 38, 41, 42, 44, 45 right, 46, 47, 48, 49, 50, 51 above, 52, 53, 54, 55, 56, 62, 63, 64, 66, 67, 69, 71 left, 74 left, 80 left, 83 right, 85 right, 86 left and above right, 87, 89, 90 above right, 91 above left and above right, 93 below left, 94, 96, 97, 99 right, 100 left, 103 right and below left, 106 left, 107 right, 109 right, 110, 111, 112 left and below right, 113 right, 119 below left, 123 right and above left, 124, 125, 126, 127, 128, 129, 130, 132, 133, 134, 135, 137, 138, 140.

N. Vermeulen, Groningen: pages 8 left, 68, 74 above right, 78 above right, 79 right, 81 right, 105 right, 117 right.